MY PALEO

Patisserie

JENNI HULET

FOREWORD BY DANIELLE WALKER

VICTORY BELT PUBLISHING

LAS VEGAS

First Published in 2015 by Victory Belt Publishing Inc.

Copyright © 2015 Jenni Hulet

ISBN-13: 978-1-628600-44-5

This book is for entertainment purposes. The publisher and author of this cookbook are not responsible in any manner whatsoever for any adverse effects arising directly or indirectly as a result of the information provided in this book.

Cover Design: Robert Milam and Chris Flynn
Cover Photography: Ashleigh Amoroso
Interior Design: Yordan Terziev and Boryana Yordanova
Interior Photography: Jenni Hulet

Printed in the U.S.A.
RRD 0115

To my parents, whose hope, resolve, humor, and unyielding passion for life have been my model for living, and without which the events that led to the creation of this book would never have become a story of redemption.

Contents

Foreword

The first time I met Jenni was sometime in early 2011. The first thing that caught my eye was her breathtaking food photography. Like Jenni, I had recently started my blog but had no experience with photography, and was having trouble getting my creations to look appetizing on the page.

On a whim, I sent her a message asking for advice on how to improve my photography. In the conversation that followed, Jenni and I were surprised to find how similar our paths to eating a grain-free diet were with regard to recovering our health. She suggested a few books and websites that could help, and we had a lengthy discussion about the pros and cons of several different cameras. While that conversation did help me with my photography, the real value that came of it was the seeds of a great friendship.

Over the years there have been countless conversations full of laughter, deep connection, and encouragement. I think that it's rare in today's virtual world to forge this kind of friendship with someone who lives so far away, but our similar passions have made our friendship effortless. Although we see each other only a few times a year, I always value my time with Jenni and look forward to her next great creation.

Naturally, when Jenni told me that she was finally going to write a book, I was thrilled! There's just something about the way she approaches her creativity that I knew would make a truly amazing book. There's a lot of similarity in how she and I approach food. Having both grown up with strong families around us, cooking and eating together as a family is a theme that's woven all throughout both of our bodies of work. We both cherish the nostalgic aspect of food and strive to preserve that in our grain-free recipe re-creations.

But I think there's something else at the heart of why this book is so unique. Jenni is a true artist. She creates more than just great recipes and stunning photography. She delves deeply into recipe creation and meticulously works and reworks them until they are just perfect. She has a relationship with her ingredients. To her, they are like living, breathing entities that she nurtures and cultivates. They are painstakingly selected and elegantly woven together until they are not just recipes—they are quite literally works of art.

Jenni approaches food, and all of life, as I've discovered, with a bold and creative reckless abandon. She has a mission to provide people with reliable recipes that will bring inspiration and art back into their kitchens, and an unyielding drive to attain it. Even in the face of physical struggles, she delivers.

With this book you are getting a little glimpse into the heart and soul of my friend Jenni. I think you'll find that it is as accessible, adventurous, and unique as she is. I encourage you to embrace the challenges you'll find in these pages. Some of these recipes may seem elaborate, but don't let that stop you. The rewards of throwing yourself into the pursuit of beauty and creativity are apparent in the enjoyment of those you are serving them to, restoring community and joy around the table.

I'm confident that you're going to love this book as much as I do. I'm proud to know Jenni and to be a part of such a great piece of work.

Danielle

—Danielle Walker
New York Times bestselling author of
Against All Grain and *Meals Made Simple*

About Jenni

Pretty much as early as I can remember, my family's culture revolved around the kitchen. I grew up in the far north part of Minnesota, and many a gray, cold, and blustery day was spent casually gathered with friends and loved ones around the kitchen table with a warm cup of coffee and a story to be shared. Some of my very earliest memories are of my parents preparing meals and welcoming guests from near and far into our home.

Our home was a place that was open to anyone and everyone, from local friends to traveling acquaintances, and there was rarely a time when we didn't have a French press full of coffee and a big pot of soup ready to warm up anybody who stopped by to say hello. For us, food was far more than sustenance for our bodies; it was the means by which people from all walks of life could come together and find common ground.

Both of my parents are avid cooks, and the unique blend of their distinct personalities created an interesting environment for me to grow up.

My mother is a kind and generous woman whose exuberance tends to spill over onto anyone who comes through our door. In our small circle, she is famous for her fresh-baked bread, and her homemade cinnamon rolls will forever live on in the minds of hundreds of transient travelers as perhaps one of the greatest culinary encounters of their lives. Coming home to the smell of a kitchen under her direction is possibly the strongest and most enduring sensation that my young memory holds.

My father is a fascinating combination of cultured intellectual and rugged mountain man: He is equally adept at teaching complex theology or catering an upscale gala as he is at field-dressing a deer or running a dogsled team across the frozen tundra. It's from him that I learned to love the vast and varied cuisines of the world, and there are very few things that brought me more joy as a young girl than getting to work side by side with him in the kitchen as he prepared the meals that welcomed so many into our home.

This unique culture lent itself well to creating a strong "sense of occasion" in my life. Because so many of the meals that we shared happened as sort of spontaneous moments to welcome surprise guests, any meal or get-together that was planned ahead of time carried with it an enhanced sense of importance. If we knew days or weeks in advance that we would be hosting friends, the sense of anticipation combined with the time to plan afforded us the ability to put together unique and elaborate meals to share with our guests. Often we would spend days planning and preparing every detail of the event.

Living in a small northern town and having a close-knit group of friends meant that more often than not, our family became the go-to choice for facilitating every wedding reception, baby shower, birthday party, and good old-fashioned neighborhood shindig that went down. Over the years, my love of serving people by creating amazing food for them became one of the most central parts of my identity. To this day there is almost nothing that I enjoy more than seeing the fulfillment of a lifelong dream sweep across a bride's face when she sees her wedding cake for the first time or watching the elation of young girls as they walk into a daddy-daughter dance that has been completely transformed into a Victorian-era ball.

When I left home at nineteen, I carried this "sense of occasion" with me, and because I married a man at twenty-two who is every bit as much of a renaissance man as my father is, the tendency to be at the center of all special events, especially when it involves food, quickly became the culture of my newly formed family as well. As we began having kids of our own and exploring our new life together, I found a new depth of expression in this idea of a "sense of occasion" as I transitioned into the role of parent. Seeing my own children come alive and take joy in this lifestyle was even more fulfilling than I could have imagined, and more so than ever I knew that this way of living life was at the core of who I am as a person.

Over the years we have made numerous wedding cakes ranging from traditional to exotic. We have catered special dinners, organized everything from elegant charity events to backyard church picnics, and had the pleasure of hosting countless people in our home. But this lifestyle that I loved, that was so central to my identity, was abruptly cut short in the winter of 2011.

Over the course of several days, my health sharply declined to the point that I was virtually paralyzed and unable to escape from persistent, excruciating pain from head to toe. Months of fruitless investigation followed, and despite the best efforts of numerous doctors and specialists, my husband and I slowly began to accept the reality that not only was the life we had built together gone, but that we may also have to seriously consider what life without me at all might look like for our young family.

In our desperation, we followed the advice of a dear friend and made an appointment with a natural doctor and nutritionist she had recommended to us. At our appointment, without any real hope in our hearts, we began to convey the sequence of events that had led us here, just as we had done so many times in the preceding six months. To our surprise, our story was not met with skepticism or vague speculation as it had been thus far. Instead, it was followed by a series of insightful questions about the subtle details of our experience that had never before been deemed valuable information by the doctors we had visited previously.

After over an hour of discussion, it was concluded that we should run some blood work to confirm the suspicion that the decline in my health was in fact due to an acute autoimmune response. The results of those tests confirmed our doctor's suspicions, and further testing revealed that my immune system was extremely unstable and that I had developed a significant sensitivity to, among other things, gluten, grains, dairy, and nightshades.

Our doctor immediately put me on an extremely restricted diet and started actively working to supplement my failing immune system to alleviate my symptoms and try to restore some balance to my broken body.

Over the course of several more weeks, I began to experience some relief from the most physically debilitating symptoms of this immune system dysfunction, but the reality of my situation also began to become clear: Because of my particular genetic disposition and the nature of this reaction, there were certain aspects of this health condition, namely my extreme food sensitivities, from which I would never fully recover.

As compared to the notion of continuing in the state in which I had been living, dealing with various food sensitivities would be an insignificant obstacle. However, for someone who has built her life around loving and giving to people through extravagant food, this news still came as quite a blow to the newly emerging glimmer of hope that I had only just begun to cling to.

Despite this fact, hope still prevailed, and we chose to move forward by embracing the challenges we were facing. We were determined to find a way to enjoy our food, however limited that prospect might be, and as a means of journaling my experience and desperately clinging to any remnant of my former creative endeavors, I decided to begin blogging about my journey.

Before my crash, I had been working as a yoga teacher and had created a blog called *The Urban Poser.* The blog was meant to be a resource for my students to receive extended instruction and for me to expand on some of the more complex and philosophical aspects of the yogic experience. Because of the physically debilitating nature of my health issues, the notion of a continuing a fully yoga-focused blog was all but gone, but since the idea of creating an entirely new blog was a bit daunting at the time, I decided to simply keep my existing setup and continue blogging about this new path.

At first, my blog posts were limited to my own experiences; they were a way for me to emotionally and philosophically process what was happening to me and my family. To be honest, to call what I was doing at that point "blogging" would be a fairly large overstatement. In the beginning, I had to dictate what I wanted to say as my husband, Ben, typed it out; though my mind was streaming with creative ideas, I was unable to hold my head up long enough to type out a blog post on my own without triggering neck spasms or severe back pain. This was truly a "spirit is willing but the flesh is weak" time of life for me.

As time passed and my recovery continued, I was eventually able to begin cooking again. Having had weeks of recovery time in which to imagine creative expressions for my newly limited diet, I hit the ground running and immediately started creating recipes. I quickly realized that I would need to start taking photos of my creations in order for people viewing my blog posts to understand what I was trying to represent, so we purchased a fifty-dollar point-and-shoot camera from Craigslist, and off I went.

During this time, a good friend of mine who had begun following my blog mentioned to me that much of what I was creating was consistent with the Paleo diet. I had heard of Paleo, but I had not looked into it at all because my primary goal over the preceding number of months, with regard to my diet, was simply to follow my doctor's instructions in order to survive.

After researching it in more depth, I began tagging my posts as Paleo and interacting with other bloggers in the Paleo community. I discovered that there was a group of generous, encouraging, and creative people who were all facing down their own unique sets of challenges with grace and enthusiasm. They welcomed me with open arms, and to this day I count many of them among a growing circle of very dear friends.

It wasn't long after this that I began to feel creatively limited by my photography skills. I was creating beautiful recipes that I was extremely enthusiastic about, but my ability to capture and represent them in all the glory that I was seeing was decidedly insufficient. I purchased my first digital SLR camera, a very used Canon 20D with a stock lens, and set my mind to learning "real" photography.

As my photography skills grew, the response to my blog posts began to increase, and I was amazed when I began to receive emails and comments from people who were trying out my recipes and enjoying my creations. I began to realize that food blogging could be a great opportunity for me to experience again that life of sharing and touching people's lives through my own love of creating beautiful food.

This realization brought a new sense of purpose and clarity to what I was doing. I knew then that despite the natural ebb and flow of my overall level of health, a lifestyle of connecting with people through sharing food, as I had done in my childhood and had carried on with my own family, was still possible. I knew that I had a choice, and that I had before me a way to truly enjoy the lifestyle that had always been "me."

But then, the choice was not really a choice at all. This is not just what I do; it's who I am.

Jenni

Why Paleo Patisserie?

When the notion of taking what I had been doing with *The Urban Poser* in the digital realm into book form first presented itself, I considered exploring a number of different expressions. Though there were many that I would love to have chosen, between the interest of my online community and a quick check of my own heart, I quickly recognized that the best and most enticing option for my first cookbook would be an exploration of my favorite topic: classic pastry making.

Rooted in a rich and varied tradition of creativity and craft, I find the art of pastry making endlessly fascinating. There's an inherent spirit of exploration that, when intermingled with the richness of many years of cultural heritage, makes for a seemingly inexhaustible set of possibilities that I never tire of.

The word *patisserie* itself has evolved over the years and across different cultures to mean a number of different things. It can refer to the prepared pastries themselves, or it can mean the shop in which they are sold. In some countries, the word is highly regulated and allowed to be used only when the proprietor of a patisserie is a licensed *maître pâtissier* (master pastry chef). In other contexts, it simply refers to desserts in a very general sense.

For the purpose of this book, I'm drawing on the general concept of patisserie to serve as a framework and launchpad for an exploration of the art of making beautiful desserts within the context of dietary limitations such as grain, gluten, and dairy sensitivities. It probably goes without saying, but this book is not about quick and easy treats to fit into your Paleo lifestyle. I don't say this to imply that all of the recipes in this book are exceedingly difficult to prepare; in fact, there are many very simple recipes to be found in these pages. What I mean is that this book is about exploring an entirely different approach to desserts, much broader in its scope and view than simply what you can and cannot eat, while still allowing you to maintain your dietary preferences.

People come to Paleo for a number of reasons. For some it is simply a choice that they've made after investigating the science and exploring how it fits into their overall concept

of health. For others, like me, it is an absolute necessity in order to manage an otherwise debilitating condition. Ultimately, though, wherever you fall in that spectrum is in many ways irrelevant because this book is not really about the "rules" and whether or not you feel like this ingredient or that one is a valid choice for any particular school of thought.

Rather, this book is about choosing to overcome the myriad forces in this life that constantly strive to divide and separate us all. It's about stepping beyond those obstacles that want to draw us away from a life of connectedness and community and moving forward in a lifestyle of embracing those things that we all have in common. These are the things that make us a society rather than just a large body of sterile, autonomous individuals with no significant connection to each other, and in my experience there are very few things as universal across culture and history as the practice of gathering around food.

FOOD AS A COMMON LANGUAGE

If you take a look at any society across the globe and throughout all of history, regardless of race, religion, economy, or geography, one thing is universally true: People celebrate. And though their celebrations may be as varied and foreign to you as their language or fashions are, one thing that is consistently true across the board is that celebration always includes, and often revolves around, food.

Every group of people in the world has their own unique expressions of elaborate, festive, and celebratory foods. These are not just recipes that they throw together each day because they need to fill their bellies. These are the traditions, shared from one generation to the next, that define them as a group, as a culture.

Celebratory foods are more than just foods; they are a common language that brings people together, despite differences of opinion or a disparity in worldview. The one thing everyone has in common is a love of their culture's unique way of celebrating, and dietary restrictions do not change this truism. With this book, I hope to give you the tools to create celebratory foods that can be shared and enjoyed by all who are gathered together, and thereby bridge the wide gap that dietary limitations create in the lives of so many people.

COMING TOGETHER

Through my own journey toward health, I've had the occasion to interact with countless others facing similar challenges, and one consistent theme that I have come across over and over again is the deep sense of loss that people feel surrounding times of celebration. Sure, people would love to have the convenience of an easy cookie here or a spontaneous treat there, but the real sense of loss that they feel resides on a much deeper level and extends far beyond simply not having something sweet to eat. There are very few things more isolating and disheartening than being unable to freely join with loved ones to celebrate significant times of life.

Whether it's a special occasion like Christmas or a birthday or simply being able to invite friends over for an evening of dinner, dessert, and conversation, we lose something fundamental when we are prevented from participating in the intentional and meaningful act of preparing and sharing beautiful, delicious desserts with the people we care about.

This book, from its ingredients and techniques to the way it is photographed and laid out, is designed to inspire and equip anyone and everyone to reclaim or discover anew their own unique sense of occasion. My sincerest desire is that whether or not entertaining friends and taking time to prepare extravagant desserts has ever been a part of your life before, this book will enable you to experience the kind of connection and fulfillment that can be found in living intentionally and taking the time to invest in the people in your life.

THE ARTISAN APPROACH

Interestingly enough, *artisan* is actually a French term that has become so commonly used in English that many people don't know it didn't originate with that tongue. As you might assume, it takes its cue from the root word *art* but differs slightly in nature from true art.

While an artist creates a tangible or intangible expression of creativity for purely aesthetic reasons, an artisan, though spurred by the same motivation, produces crafts that, though they may be as aesthetically pleasing as strict "art," are designed primarily to serve a practical function.

The reason the idea of an artisan approach matters is that whether your choice to eat Paleo is an internal conviction or something that has been externally imposed by circumstances beyond your control, the simple fact is that our instinctive human response to limitation is almost always pragmatism. If we are faced with an inability to do what we have always done, in this case eating a certain way, our natural response is to say, "Well, what *can* I eat, then?"

This question predisposes us to begin making choices based on a very practical metric: namely, does this food satisfy the need for sustenance, emotional comfort, or personal identity while still adhering to whatever motivation brought us to this dietary choice to begin with? Unfortunately, in the face of these three very powerful needs, the more subtle values of appreciating beauty, fostering creativity, connecting socially, and observing a sense of occasion all too often become marginalized, demonized, or overlooked entirely. But make no mistake, these needs are equally essential when the goal of life is to be a healthy, well-rounded, and balanced individual. To dismiss them out of simple pragmatism would be a tremendous loss of the very values that all truly great societies have been based on.

If this all sounds a bit too heady for you, don't worry; the simple fact is that the difference between a pragmatic approach and an artisan approach ultimately boils down to two simple things: intention and effort.

MAKE IT YOUR OWN

If there's one thing that I have discovered in living with dietary limitations and raising two very unique boys with their own unique sets of food sensitivities, it's this: Limitations don't feel quite so much like limitations if you find a way to make it special. I like to think of this as the "cherry on top" approach, because even the simplest things can feel special if you take the time to dress them up a little. I love the quote, "The difference between ordinary and extraordinary is that little extra."

I'm not suggesting that every single thing you eat needs to become a huge production, but the simple fact is that we humans are hardwired to appreciate beauty, and it's a rare person who is not at least a little bit moved when someone goes out of their way to show them a little personal consideration.

This is what I mean by intention and effort: not excessive labor and contrivance, but rather simple, personal consideration. Does your daughter love strawberries? Take the time to slice and fan out a few strawberries on top of her dessert. Are the friends who are coming over for dinner coffee aficionados? Consider making an espresso mousse to top some ice cream or crush some coffee beans to sprinkle on top. Does your celebration revolve around a specific holiday? Think about more than just the traditional desserts, but also the colors, flavors, and themes that surround that holiday, and find a way to creatively incorporate them into your family's traditions. Every time you put special touches on a dessert, you elevate it to an artisan food.

Given the incredibly wide variety of health issues that each and every reader of this book might have, compounded by the vast uniqueness of our individual tastes, it would be incredibly difficult to create a catalog of recipes that could meet each and every individual's tastes and needs. So, though I've included a number of my favorite combinations that range from very classic to decidedly outside the box, my intention in doing so was not just to provide a limited list of options for you to reproduce. Though I think you will love these recipes, my hope is that you will view this book as both a source of inspiration and as a painter's color palette, with your life as the blank canvas.

Think of this book a bit like those old "choose your own adventure" books. The recipes and techniques included here are intended to provide the inspiration and tools that you need to create your own unique, beautiful, and meaningful expressions, regardless of the dietary limitations you might have. For example, you will find recipes for glazes, frostings, and fillings and for cakes, crusts, choux pastry, and more, which you can to mix and match to cobble together your own unique creations.

If all you get from this book is a short, fixed list of recipes to add to your normal rotation, that's fine, but if that were the case, I would feel a bit like I had failed to accomplish my goal. Ultimately, my primary objective is to encourage and equip you to charge headlong into the adventure of making desserts with a fresh sense of unfettered exuberance and unlimited potential.

I hope these pages will inspire you to take ownership of this aspect of your life—to feel the freedom to embrace the challenge and make it your own. What I mean is, if there's a recipe in this book—or anywhere, for that matter—that you would like to make, but its ingredients don't fit with your or your family's limitations, don't write that recipe off as something you can't enjoy; just get creative and make your own version of it! Do you want to make one of my desserts that is based on an almond flour cake, but you can't have almonds? Use a coconut flour cake instead, even if it's not one of mine! There are so many great books and talented bloggers out there that there's no reason you can't take an idea from these pages and use recipes from other sources that you've come to trust to make a version of my recipe that works for your family. That's not a compromise or somehow lesser in any way…that's the goal!

Orson Welles once said, "The enemy of art is the absence of limitations." What he meant was that genuine creativity is almost always borne out of the desire to overcome a limitation. It's the nature of true art, and my sincere desire is that this book will help lay the foundation for your creativity to flourish as you learn to live beyond your own dietary limitations.

Getting Started

Before charging headlong into one of the recipes in this book, which might leave you wondering why your labors didn't result in the perfect cake, tart, or cream puffs you were hoping for, I recommend taking a moment to read the baking tips that follow, as well as the section on how weights and measurements are used in this book.

Making beautiful and delicious pastries can take some practice. My motto is, "Recipes don't make beautiful and tasty desserts; people do." In the end, when you see the faces of your friends and family light up with awe and enthusiasm, all the effort is worth it.

HELPFUL TIPS

I wouldn't go so far as to say that these are "rules," but when it comes to pastry making, I have found that minding a few minor guidelines goes a long way toward helping you produce great-looking and great-tasting desserts.

Set up your space. Call it a mystery if you like, but I've always found that if my kitchen is cluttered and crazy, it somehow comes through in my pastries. I'm not a super-organized baker to begin with, and things always end up being pretty messy. But as long as I start with a little organization, things always seem to go better for me.

Have the right tools. You don't need ultra-fancy tools and a large, super-decked-out workspace, but you do need to have the tools you're going to use for a recipe. The old saying goes, "Every job is easy if you have the right tools," and that's absolutely true with pastry making.

Always preheat the oven before you do anything else. For even baking, a standard oven takes a minimum of 15 minutes to preheat, regardless of when it beeps and says that it's at the right temperature. I always use an oven thermometer as well, because I have yet to find an oven that reads at the correct temperature all the time.

Prepare for making the recipe. Always start by taking a moment to read through the entire recipe. Make sure that you have the ingredients in the right amounts and that your tools are clean and accessible. Measure and weigh the specific amounts of ingredients you'll need for the recipe, using as many prep bowls as necessary. Precut the parchment paper, grease the pans, and so on. Many recipes are time-sensitive, and success depends on having what you need when you need it.

When baking, never leave the kitchen for very long. Pastry making requires you to use a measure of intuition, and you have to stay engaged in the process if you want great results. What I mean is that if you have to bake something for 25 minutes, it's unwise to leave the kitchen and return after 24 minutes hoping to find a perfect cake waiting for you. For certain recipes with shorter baking times, like sponge cakes, I actually don't leave the kitchen at all. For longer baking recipes, I try to be back in the kitchen at least 10 minutes before the expected baking time is over to allow for recipes that are done sooner than expected.

Be patient. It's a virtue, after all. Don't be anxious; if a recipe says to whip something for 15 minutes, don't stop at 13, unless you've done it enough times to know for sure that it is ready early.

Respect the cool-down process. Cooling time is a critical part of most recipes; it should be thought of as part of the baking/cooking process. This is especially true with coconut flour cakes, which tend to require the full cooling time for the internal texture not to be soggy.

WEIGHT VERSUS VOLUME

There are two basic approaches to handling ingredient measurements: by weight and by volume. In the United States, the typical home cook uses volume to measure ingredients, with standardized cups for dry and wet ingredients. Outside the U.S., it is far more common to measure ingredients by metric weight (using a scale) or by using a combination of weight and volume.

The primary benefits of measuring by weight are ease and consistency. For example, if you scoop out a cup of flour three times, you will likely get three slightly different amounts. However, measuring your flour in grams ensures that you will always use the exact amount the recipe calls for. These variations may not seem like a big deal, but in many recipes they can mean the difference between success and failure. Measuring ingredients with a scale helps to minimize the potential for error and makes combining ingredients in one bowl as simple as hitting the tare button before the addition of each new ingredient. I also find that using grams instead of ounces makes it easier to keep track when combining ingredients, because I don't have to mentally convert the amounts when the number of ounces goes above 16 and the scale reads 1 pound instead.

All of the recipes in this book have been developed using measurements based on weight (grams) for dry ingredients and volume (cups and milliliters) for liquids. I've also included the amounts of dry ingredients in cups and tablespoons for convenience, but for best results, I highly suggest that you use a scale to measure dry ingredients.

If you still prefer to use standardized cups and tablespoons, please pay special attention to the details in the instructions, such as "lightly packed" and "slightly rounded," because observing these details will help you produce the closest results to the method using weight.

Note: It is important to know that "standardized" cups and tablespoons differ in different parts of the world. For example, an American liquid measuring cup holds 240 milliliters, whereas the slightly larger UK and Australian cups hold 250 milliliters. So if you are cooking by volume using non-American cups and tablespoons, you will need to do some research to determine what adjustments you will need to make.

Ingredients

EGGS

For this book, I use the standard U.S. large egg, which weighs 57 grams (in the shell). The Australian standard for a large egg can be anywhere from 50 to 58 grams, and Europe lists a large egg as being up to a whopping 73 grams, which is even larger than a U.S. extra-large! While this may not seem like a lot of difference in a single egg, this variance can mean the difference between success and failure in recipes that use a large number of eggs or that are dependent on highly absorbent ingredients such as coconut flour. So if this concerns you, please research the standard egg sizing for your country.

Storing Egg Whites and Yolks

To freeze egg whites: Pour each egg white into one well of an ice cube tray and freeze, then transfer to a freezer bag. All you need to do is defrost them at room temperature when they're called for.

To freeze egg yolks: Thoroughly mix 1 teaspoon of sugar with each egg yolk before freezing using the same method as the whites; this will keep the egg proteins fluid after freezing. When using these frozen egg yolks in a recipe, remember to subtract a teaspoon of sugar for every egg yolk used.

American Egg Size Chart

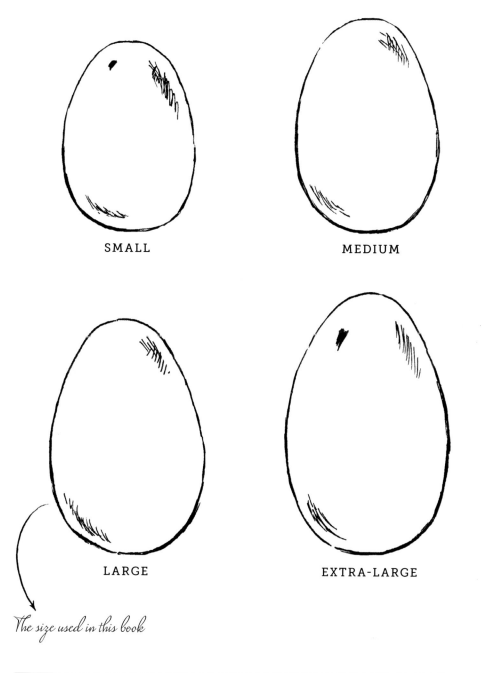

SMALL

MEDIUM

LARGE

EXTRA-LARGE

The size used in this book

The Anatomy of a Large U.S. Egg

In shell = 57 g   Out of shell = 50 g   Egg yolk = 18 g   Egg white = 30 g

FLOURS

Nut Flours and Meals

Nut flours used in this book include blanched almond flour (meaning without skins) as well as pistachio and hazelnut flours. The finer the grind of the flours, the better the texture your baked goods will have. Ideally, the texture will be powdery and fine enough that the flour can be pressed through a fine-mesh sieve (not to be confused with a traditional flour sifter).

Almond flour has become readily available from a number of sources. **Pistachio and hazelnut flours** can be harder to find, but can easily be made at home by pulsing chopped nuts in a small grinder till they reach the consistency described above. Nut meals can also be used but are considerably more coarse than flours, though the desired consistency can be achieved by using this same method. See page 294 for my preferred brands.

If measuring flour by volume (cups) to make the recipes in this book, I recommend using the "scoop and sweep" method for the most accurate results. Simply scoop up a slightly rounded cup of flour and then level the flour by sliding a flat edge across the top of the cup.

Nut-Free Flours and Starches

Coconut flour is a great nut-free flour alternative for grain-free baking. It is super absorbent and loves moisture. For this reason, you will find that the amount of coconut flour used in recipes is much smaller as compared to other baking flours. Recipes containing coconut flour also rely heavily on eggs and liquids to create volume and lightness.

Arrowroot and tapioca flours are the two starchy flours used in this book. I use them mainly for adding lightness to cakes and crispness to cookies and crusts. Arrowroot flour has a more neutral taste than tapioca, but for the purposes of this book, they can be used interchangeably. In some cases, they can substitute for traditional wheat flour in choux pastry and sponge cake recipes.

SWEETENERS

Honey is a great natural and nutritious liquid sweetener. It lends moisture and even browning power to baked goods. Because honey can have a strong flavor and color, I like to stick with the lighter varieties, such as clover or orange. But any local honey will do. Try to buy from sources you trust.

Organic maple syrup is another delicious and natural liquid sweetener. Though some people have been led to believe that "Grade B" is the less refined and more nutritious of the maple syrup options, in reality there is no difference between the grades. You can choose lighter grades for a mellow flavor or darker ones for a pronounced maple flavor.

Organic maple sugar is a type of granulated sugar that is made from the sap of the maple tree. There are many recipes available for making homemade maple sugar, which can be useful if you do not have access to commercial maple sugar. Depending on your source, making your own can also be more affordable, but this is not always the case.

The main thing to be aware of is that homemade maple sugar weighs less per cup (volume) than most store-bought, granulated varieties. To get consistent results from the recipes in this book, it is best to weigh it or to firmly pack your measuring cups.

For the **powdered sugar** used in this book's recipes, simply combine 1 cup (200 g) of firmly packed maple sugar with 1 tablespoon of arrowroot flour and blend in a high-powered blender (like a Blendtec) till the sugar turns into a very fine powder. This will produce 1½ cups of powdered sugar. Do not pack powdered sugar when measuring by volume.

COCONUT PRODUCTS

Coconut milk. For the purposes of this book, when I use coconut milk I'm referring to canned, full-fat coconut milk. Store leftover coconut milk in a covered jar in the fridge for up to 4 or 5 days, or freeze it in ice cube trays for later use.

Coconut cream (from canned, full-fat coconut milk). When I refer to coconut cream in this book, I'm talking about the thick cream that has separated and risen to the top of a can of chilled full-fat coconut milk. A standard 13½-ounce (400-ml) can of full-fat coconut milk yields approximately ½ cup (120 ml) to ¾ cup (180 ml) of coconut cream. Guar gum–based coconut milks tend to produce the most stable and silky whipped cream.

Coconut butter (manna). Coconut butter is made from fresh whole coconut flesh (not just the oil). In this book it is used to make glazes. Make sure that the oil is fully incorporated before using. If needed, warm the jar till the coconut butter becomes stirrable. Simply place the jar in a pot of warm water till the coconut butter is soft.

FATS AND OILS

Sustainable organic palm shortening. One of the great things about palm shortening is that it is not hydrogenated, contains no trans fats, and is odorless and neutral in flavor. This makes it perfect for baking. The palm shortening used in this book is both sustainable and rainforest friendly. For recommended brands, see page 295.

Ghee (clarified butter). Ghee has a rich, centuries-long history as a staple in Indian cooking. The benefit of using ghee is that it is extremely low in, and often completely free of, lactose and casein, the two main offenders when it comes to dairy allergies.

The majority of the recipes in this book use palm shortening and ghee interchangeably. There are minor differences in how these two fats behave in certain baked goods, but they are negligible. The main difference is that ghee weighs slightly more than shortening, as you can see in the charts on pages 297–298. This difference becomes more noticeable when a recipe calls for ½ cup or more of shortening or ghee. To account for this weight difference when using ghee and measuring by volume (cups), simply reduce the amount of fat by ¼ cup for every full cup called for in the recipe. However, if you use a scale to weigh shortening or ghee, there is no need to consider these differences in cup amounts.

CACAO PRODUCTS

Nonalkalized cocoa powder. This is a natural product made from pure cacao beans that have been fermented, dried, roasted, and ground. Cocoa powder known as Dutch process cocoa has been treated with an alkali to neutralize the acidity. The recipes in this book use nonalkalized cocoa only.

Chocolate. There are many varieties and forms of chocolate. For most baking applications, any good-quality chocolate will work. For making ganache and for melting and coating, chocolate with a cacao content of at least 70 percent will produce the best results.

OTHER INGREDIENTS

Berry powder. In this book, I use freeze-dried berries, finely ground and sifted, to add flavor and color. Whole dried berries can be purchased in many health food stores and online and then ground to a fine powdery texture using a spice or coffee grinder.

A 2-ounce (56 g) bag of freeze-dried raspberries yields approximately 6 tablespoons (12 g) of sifted berry powder.

Gelatin. Gelatin is graded by "bloom," which is a measure of stiffness and strength. The powdered gelatin commonly found in the U.S. is usually 225 bloom, whereas sheet/leaf gelatin comes in a variety of blooms. For this book I use a 225-bloom powdered gelatin from a high-quality source such as Great Lakes.

The process of converting the amount of powdered gelatin called for in recipes to leaf/sheet gelatin and vice versa can be tricky and often is unreliable. For best results, I recommend ordering the Great Lakes brand of powdered gelatin online.

Equipment

BAKEWARE

Cake pans. For cakes I use mainly 6-inch (15-cm) and occasionally 4-inch (10-cm) round cake pans, unless otherwise stated. I prefer smaller layer cakes because grain-free ingredients are very nutrient-dense and expensive. A cake this size actually goes pretty far, typically feeding eight or more people.

Tart pans. The primary difference between tart pans and traditional pie pans is the shape and depth of the sides. Tart pans typically have straight, sometimes fluted sides that give a more finished look than the typically sloped sides of pie pans. They also tend to be shallower. Tart pans with a diameter of 4 inches (10 cm) or larger usually have a removable bottom that allows you to slide the outside ring off of the tart without affecting the crust.

The tart pans that I use most in this book are 9-inch (23-cm), 5-inch (12.75-cm), and 3-inch (7.5-cm) round pans and a 12-well, 2½-inch (6.5-cm) mini tart pan.

Cookie sheets. Cookie sheets do not have raised edges and offer a large surface area for making cookies, piping dough and meringues, and so on. The standard cookie sheet found in stores generally measures 13 by 18 inches (33 by 46 cm), which is the perfect size for most home ovens.

Jelly roll pan. A jelly roll pan, also known as a sheet pan, is a rectangular, rimmed baking sheet. For the recipes in this book, you will need a 15 by 10 by 1-inch (38 by 25 by 2.5-cm) jelly roll pan.

Madeleine pan. This baking pan is designed for making the classic French cakes with a traditional scalloped shape (see pages 160–165). I use a nonstick, stainless-steel, 12-cavity pan with 3¼-inch (8.25-cm)-long madeleine molds.

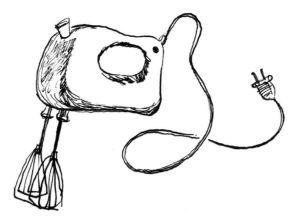

APPLIANCES

Oven. The stated baking times for all of the recipes in this book are based on a conventional oven. If using a convection oven, make the necessary adjustments.

Stand mixer or hand mixer. In most cases, using a stand mixer is preferable because it minimizes your workload and makes it easier to add hot sugar syrups and other ingredients while beating. If necessary, a hand mixer will get the job done. In a few cases, such as the Sabayon recipe on page 261, I prefer a hand mixer, but that information is noted within the recipes.

Digital scale. I prefer to use a digital scale when baking. It improves accuracy, and converting from ounces to grams is as simple as pressing a button. See page 26 for more on the issue of measuring by weight versus measuring by volume (cups).

Spice/coffee grinder. A grinder is useful for everything from making berry powders to grinding nuts.

Automatic ice cream maker. For making the dairy-free ice creams in this book, a 1½-quart (1.4-L) automatic ice cream maker is ideal. This inexpensive appliance is simple to use.

Pizzelle maker. Pizzelles are traditional thin cookies made in a machine not unlike a waffle maker. They come in both large and small sizes. In this book I use the small 4½-inch (11.5-cm) size to make cannoli-style cookies (page 215) and small waffle cones (pages 212 and 213).

OTHER TOOLS

Fine-mesh sieve. Large (8 inches/20 cm) for sifting flour and straining pastry creams, curds, and more; and small (3 inches/7.5 cm) for dusting and decorating with sugars.

Mechanical ice cream scoops. Depending on the size and brand, these scoops are sometimes referred to as cookie scoops. They feature a lever that allows you to cleanly release whatever it is you are scooping. I use three sizes in this book: mini (2 teaspoons, 1¼-inch/3-cm diameter); small (1½ tablespoons, 1¾-inch/4.5-cm diameter); and medium (4 tablespoons/60 ml, 2-inch/5-cm diameter).

Pastry bags and tips. You will need one or two large (16-inch/40.5-cm) pastry bags to be fitted with the following tips:
- ⅜-inch (1-cm) plain round tip (Ateco 804 [size 4]/Wilton 10)—for piping grissini
- ⅜-inch (1-cm) French star tip (Ateco 864 [size 4]/Wilton 32)—for small decorations
- ½-inch (1.25-cm) plain round tip (Ateco 806 [size 6]/Wilton 1A)—for piping cream puffs and éclairs
- ½-inch (1.25-cm) open star tip (Ateco 826 [size 6]/Wilton 1M)—for creating nice ruffles when piping frosting and whipped cream
- Bismarck tip (Ateco 230/Wilton 230)—for filling éclairs and cream puffs

Rolling pin guide rings. These silicone rings fit on the outside of your rolling pin to allow for even rolling of dough. See pages 274–275 for photo instructions.

Saucepans (heavy-bottomed). Small (1.5 quarts/1.4 L) and medium (3 quarts/2.8 L).

Small offset spatula. Sometimes referred to as a palette knife, an offset spatula has an angled blade for spreading fillings and frostings evenly. A spatula with a 4- to 6-inch (10- to 15-cm) blade is ideal.

Thermometer. A traditional candy or digital thermometer is critical for making caramel, custards, meringues, and jams. I have a three-second instant-read digital Thermapen by ThermoWorks. It is one of the best kitchen investments I've ever made.

How to Use This Book

In my grandmother's kitchen there's a small box that sits on the windowsill. It's made of hard gray plastic and is just large enough to hold about one hundred 5 by 7-inch note cards. The box itself is nothing special; it's a durable container that can be purchased in just about any store in the world. The contents of this box, however, are quite literally priceless.

My grandmother's recipe box contains dozens of recipes that have been cultivated and refined over the decades. They have stood the test of time, making appearances at holidays, birthdays, and special events throughout the course of my life, as well as the generations before mine.

In a time when looking for a recipe is as easy as pulling up a web browser, the notion of breaking out an old recipe box can seem a bit antiquated, but as any baker will tell you, finding recipes that you can depend on is an essential part of becoming a versatile and consistent cook. So whether they are housed in a box like my grandmother's or are just a bunch of bookmarks in your browser, building a collection of recipes that are your go-to staples is a great way to develop as a baker. And ultimately, this idea is the premise and purpose of this whole book.

The first two chapters are all about giving you access to fundamental building blocks that will be referenced throughout the rest of this book. Much like my grandmother's recipe box, these fillings, frosting, glazes, and more are the recipes that you will return to again and again as you make the pastries in this book. The rest of the book contains base recipes for cakes and pastries that can be dressed up in countless ways using the recipes found in chapters 1 and 2, along with some of my favorite combinations.

Because these recipes are intended to be used in a number of different applications, they sometimes yield slightly more than is required for a particular recipe. I've done my best to indicate this within the recipes as well as to include storage instructions for any extra you might have. In my house, those small amounts of extra filling are the "bonus" that my kids get to enjoy as I work on whatever it is that I'm making.

The purpose is fun and the possibilities are endless, so dive in and explore them.

Chapter 1:

FILLINGS & MORE

PASTRY CREAMS

Traditional pastry creams use starch to achieve their thick and creamy texture. For this recipe, I borrow from the method of preparing Bavarian cream and use gelatin to set the cream instead. I find that this produces a nice pastry cream that is both stable and versatile.

Pastry Cream

INGREDIENTS

2 teaspoons powdered gelatin

2 tablespoons cold water

4 large egg yolks

⅓ cup (80 ml) maple syrup or honey

1½ cups (375 ml) full-fat coconut milk

2 teaspoons vanilla extract (omit for flavor variations)

SPECIAL EQUIPMENT

Candy thermometer

YIELD

About 1 cup (240 ml)

METHOD

1. In small bowl, sprinkle the gelatin over the cold water and allow it to soften (bloom) while you prepare the rest of the ingredients.

2. In a large heatproof bowl, whisk together the eggs and maple syrup till well combined and frothy.

3. In a medium-sized saucepan over medium heat, bring the coconut milk just to a boil. Slowly pour it into the egg mixture, whisking constantly to prevent the eggs from coagulating. Pour the whole mixture back into the saucepan and cook over medium heat, stirring continuously, till it thickens to the consistency of heavy cream and reaches 160°F (71°C) on a candy thermometer, about 7 minutes.

4. Remove from the heat and whisk in the vanilla, if using. Pour the mixture through a fine-mesh sieve into a clean bowl. Whisk in the prepared gelatin. Cover and chill for a few hours till thick and set.

5. When ready to use, remove from the fridge and beat till smooth. The pastry cream can be kept chilled in a covered container for several days.

Flavor Variations for Pastry Cream:

Banana Pastry Cream

INGREDIENTS

1 recipe Pastry Cream, modified as described

1 medium banana, peeled

2 teaspoons banana liqueur (optional)

METHOD

In a blender, purée the coconut milk called for in the Pastry Cream recipe together with the banana till smooth. Strain the milk using a fine-mesh sieve. Then follow the instructions above, substituting the banana-flavored milk for the plain coconut milk and the banana liqueur (if using) for the vanilla.

Matcha Green Tea Pastry Cream

INGREDIENTS

1 recipe Pastry Cream, modified as described

3 tablespoons matcha green tea powder

METHOD

Heat the coconut milk called for in the Pastry Cream recipe in a saucepan over medium-high heat. As soon as the milk comes to a boil, remove the pan from the heat and whisk in the green tea powder till well combined. Allow to cool to room temperature. Then follow the instructions for the Pastry Cream recipe, substituting the green tea–flavored milk for the plain coconut milk.

Pistachio Pastry Cream

INGREDIENTS

1 recipe Pastry Cream, modified as described

½ cup (60 g) pistachio flour

A few drops of almond extract

2 teaspoons almond or pistachio liqueur (optional)

METHOD

1. Heat the coconut milk called for in the Pastry Cream recipe in a saucepan over medium-high heat. As soon as the milk comes to a boil, remove the pan from the heat and stir in the pistachio flour. Set aside to steep for 10 minutes. Pour the mixture into a blender and blend till smooth. Strain the milk through a fine-mesh sieve and let cool to room temperature. If this does not quite yield a full 1½ cups (375 ml), simply add a bit of plain coconut milk to make up the difference.

2. Follow the instructions for the Pastry Cream recipe, substituting the pistachio-flavored milk for the plain coconut milk and the almond extract and liqueur, if using, for the vanilla.

Praline Pastry Cream

INGREDIENTS

1 recipe Pastry Cream, modified as described

½ cup (120 ml) Praline Paste (page 69)

2 teaspoons Frangelico liqueur (optional)

METHOD

Follow the instructions for the Pastry Cream recipe with the following modifications. When first heating the coconut milk in step 3, whisk in the praline paste, making a praline-flavored milk. In step 4, substitute the Frangelico liqueur for the vanilla if desired.

Whipped Coconut Cream

To make coconut cream, place a can of full-fat coconut milk in the refrigerator for 24 to 48 hours. Remove the cream, leaving as much of the water behind as possible. (Reserve the coconut water; you may need it to lighten the whipped cream.) One 13½-ounce (400-ml) can of chilled, full-fat coconut milk typically yields ½ to ¾ cup (120 to 180 ml) of coconut cream. Once whipped, this can increase in volume to between ¾ and 1 cup (180 and 240 ml).

Sweetened Whipped Cream

INGREDIENTS

Cold coconut cream from 1 (13½-ounce/400-ml) can full-fat coconut milk (see above)

1 to 2 tablespoons maple syrup or honey, or to taste

½ teaspoon vanilla extract

YIELD

¾ to 1 cup (180 to 240 ml)

METHOD

1. Place the coconut cream in the bowl of a stand mixer fitted with a whisk attachment (or use a metal bowl and a hand mixer).

2. Beat on high speed for 1 to 3 minutes, till thick and voluminous. Turn the mixer down to low and add the maple syrup and vanilla. Turn the mixer back up to high speed and beat again till fluffy and thick.

NOTE

If the coconut cream is very thick and not increasing in volume, add small amounts of the reserved coconut water, 1 teaspoon at a time, till it lightens and begins to increase in volume. Be careful to not add too much, though, as the cream can become runny.

Flavor Variations for Sweetened Whipped Cream:

NOTE

For all flavor variations, increase the amount of liquid sweetener by 1 tablespoon.

Chocolate Whipped Cream.

Follow the recipe for Sweetened Whipped Cream, but add 3 tablespoons of cocoa powder to the whipped cream in step 2, when the sweetener is added. Before adding the cocoa, turn the mixer to low speed, and keep it on low till the cocoa is incorporated.

Raspberry Whipped Cream.

Follow the recipe for Sweetened Whipped Cream, but add 2 to 3 tablespoons of raspberry powder (see page 37) to the whipped cream in step 2, when the sweetener is added. Before adding the berry powder, turn the mixer to low speed, and keep it on low till the powder is incorporated.

Matcha Green Tea Whipped Cream.

Follow the recipe for Sweetened Whipped Cream, but add 1 tablespoon of matcha green tea powder to the whipped cream in step 2, when the sweetener is added. Taste and add up to 1 tablespoon more matcha green tea powder if desired. Before adding the matcha powder, turn the mixer to low speed, and keep it on low till the powder is incorporated.

Espresso Whipped Cream.

Follow the recipe for Sweetened Whipped Cream, but add 1½ teaspoons of instant espresso coffee or espresso powder to the whipped cream in step 2, when the sweetener is added. Taste and add an additional 1½ teaspoons of instant espresso coffee or espresso powder if desired.

JAMS

Jams make delicious fillings for cakes, éclairs, and tarts. All jam recipes can be made with fresh or frozen fruit, but I prefer fresh fruit whenever possible. Feel free to double these recipes. Jams can be kept in the fridge for up to a week or frozen for up to a few months. I don't recommend canning because of the lower sugar content of these recipes.

Orange Marmalade

This recipe can be made with either sweet or bitter oranges or a combination of both. Personal taste and seasonal availability are the primary factors in choosing your oranges.

INGREDIENTS

1 pound (455 g) oranges of choice

1 medium lemon

3 cups (710 ml) water

2 cups (475 ml) maple syrup or honey

SPECIAL EQUIPMENT

Candy thermometer

Cloth tea bag

YIELD

About 2 cups/1 pint (475 ml)

METHOD

1. Wash and dry the oranges and lemon and cut them in half crosswise. Remove the seeds, place them in a cloth tea bag, and set aside. (The seeds provide extra pectin.)

2. Cut each of the orange and lemon halves into quarters, giving you 8 pieces per fruit. Turn each piece so that the rind is facing up. Thinly slice each of the eighths crosswise and transfer the slices and juices to a large saucepan. (This will create a marmalade with discernible pieces of rind; if you like marmalade with a smoother texture, finely chop the citrus peel instead.) Add the water and bag of seeds and bring to a boil. Boil for 5 minutes, then turn off the heat, cover, and let cool. Place the pan in the refrigerator and chill for at least 8 hours or overnight. This helps to pull the pectin out of the oranges.

3. Place a small plate in the freezer. Remove the orange mixture from the fridge and bring it to a simmer, uncovered, over medium-high heat. Reduce the heat to keep the mixture at a simmer and cook till the peel is tender, about 15 minutes. Stir in the maple syrup and bring the mixture back to a boil, stirring periodically to prevent burning. Cook till the mixture reaches 220°F (104°C) on a candy thermometer. This usually takes 30 to 40 minutes.

4. To test for doneness, remove the plate from the freezer and place a little jam on it. Return it to the freezer for a minute. If it has a thickness when pushed with a finger, it's done. If it's runny and spreads out over the plate, it needs to cook longer.

5. Remove from the heat and pour into a heatproof 1-pint (475-ml) jar. Allow to cool before covering and placing in the fridge. Chill for a few hours before using.

Apricot Jam

INGREDIENTS

1½ pounds (680 g) apricots

¼ cup (60 ml) water

1½ cups (375 ml) maple syrup or honey

1 teaspoon lemon juice

SPECIAL EQUIPMENT

Candy thermometer

YIELD

About 2 cups/1 pint (475 ml)

METHOD

1. Wash and pat dry the apricots. Cut them in half and remove the kernels, then cut them in half again.

2. Place the apricots and water in a medium-sized saucepan over medium heat. Cook, covered, stirring frequently, till tender, 10 to 15 minutes.

3. Add the maple syrup and lemon juice and cook over medium-high heat, uncovered. Skim off any foam that surfaces. Stir often as the mixture thickens so it doesn't burn. Continue to cook till the jam reads 220°F (104°C) on a candy thermometer. It should appear jellylike.

4. Remove from the heat and pour into a heatproof 1-pint (475-ml) jar. Allow to cool before covering and placing in the fridge. Chill for a few hours before using.

Blackberry or Raspberry Jam

INGREDIENTS

1½ pounds (680 g) blackberries or raspberries (about 4 cups)

⅓ cup (80 ml) water or red wine

⅔ cup (160 ml) maple syrup or honey, or more to taste*

1 tablespoon lemon juice

The amount of sweetener used depends on the ripeness of the fruit.

YIELD

About 1 cup (240 ml)

METHOD

1. Place the berries and water in a small saucepan over medium heat. Cook, covered, for a few minutes, till the berries start to release some of their water. Mash them with a fork.

2. Add the maple syrup and lemon juice and bring to a boil over medium-high heat. Cook till the mixture starts to thicken, stirring often toward the end of cooking. You'll know it's about done when you pull the spoon across the bottom of the pan and it takes a few seconds for the jam to fill in the space.

3. Remove from the heat and pour into a heatproof 8-ounce (240-ml) jar. Allow to cool before covering and placing in the fridge. Chill for a few hours before using.

CURDS

Curds are creamy, egg yolk–based fillings that come in many flavors. Their fresh and often tart taste makes them a perfect base for fruit tarts, as well as a delicious filling for sweet cakes.

Lemon Curd

INGREDIENTS

½ cup (120 ml) lemon juice

½ cup (120 ml) maple syrup or honey

3 large egg yolks

2 large eggs

Pinch of salt

6 tablespoons (72 g) palm shortening or ghee

SPECIAL EQUIPMENT

Candy thermometer

YIELD

About 1 cup (240 ml)

METHOD

1. Set aside a medium-sized bowl and a fine-mesh sieve. Bring about 2 inches (5 cm) of water to a simmer in a medium-sized saucepan.

2. In a large heatproof bowl, whi... together the lemon juice, maple syrup, egg yolks, whole eggs, and salt. Whisk in the shortening by the tablespoon, then place the bowl over the simmering water and continue whisking till completely melted. Continue heating the mixture, whisking constantly, till it thickens and reaches about 170°F (76°C) on a candy thermometer, 7 to 10 minutes.

3. Pour the curd through the fine-mesh sieve and chill. It will thicken further as it cools. Store the curd in a covered container in the fridge for up to a week.

VARIATION: PASSION FRUIT CURD

Replace the lemon juice with ½ cup (120 ml) of passion fruit pulp with seeds.

Note: Passion fruit pulp with or without seeds can often be purchased frozen. To make ½ cup (120 ml) of fresh passion fruit pulp with seeds, you will need approximately ¾ pound (340 g) of passion fruit (between 7 and 10 medium-sized fruits). Cut the fruits in half and scoop out the flesh. Press through a fine-mesh sieve to remove any thick pulp. This will also separate the seeds. Pick out the seeds, then rinse the seeds and, if desired, add them to the strained passion fruit pulp.

Zabaglione

Traditional tiramisù combines zabaglione with mascarpone cheese to create a thick filling. Because the Tiramisù recipe in this book is dairy-free, a different approach is necessary to achieve the required texture. Here I use a combination of gelatin and thick coconut cream to accomplish that goal.

INGREDIENTS

1½ teaspoons powdered gelatin

1 tablespoon cold water

⅔ cup (160 ml) maple syrup

12 large egg yolks

1 cup (240 ml) Marsala wine

Cold coconut cream from 2 (13½-ounce/400-ml) cans of chilled, full-fat coconut milk (see page 48)

SPECIAL EQUIPMENT

Candy thermometer

YIELD

About 4 cups (1 L)

METHOD

1. In a small ramekin, sprinkle the gelatin over the cold water and leave to bloom while you prepare the rest of the recipe.

2. Bring about 2 inches (5 cm) of water to a simmer in a medium-sized saucepan. In a large heatproof bowl, whisk together the maple syrup and egg yolks till pale and slightly thickened. Then whisk in the wine.

3. Set the bowl over the pan of simmering water. It is important that the bottom of the bowl does not touch the water. This setup is often called a *bain-marie* and works similarly to a double boiler. With a hand mixer or an immersion blender fitted with a whisk attachment, beat the mixture constantly while it heats over the water. Use a mixer speed that won't throw sauce all over the room. If you need to stop beating for any reason, remove the bowl from the water and return it when ready to resume whipping. Otherwise, the eggs will cook too fast and curdle.

4. Continue beating till the mixture has the consistency of whipped cream and reaches 160°F (71°C) degrees on a candy thermometer. Remove the saucepan from the heat, then remove the bowl from the saucepan and discard the hot water. Place the bloomed gelatin in the saucepan, allowing the residual heat to melt it. Whisk the melted gelatin into the warm sauce, loosely cover the bowl, and chill for about 40 minutes, till cooled but not fully set.

5. When the mixture is cool, beat the cold coconut cream in a large metal bowl for a few minutes, till voluminous and light. Whisk the cream into the cooled sauce till fully combined. Use as directed for the Tiramisù recipe on page 159.

Chapter 2:

FROSTINGS & GLAZES

Swiss Meringue

This meringue is easy to make, and its lovely, velvety texture pipes well. It is also the base for Swiss Meringue Buttercream (page 58). Because the egg whites in this style of meringue are heated to 160°F (71°C), it is considered food-safe.

The addition of cream of tartar helps to stabilize the whipped egg whites, makes the meringue more voluminous, and reduces the risk of overbeating. It can be omitted or replaced with an equal amount of lemon juice, but cream of tartar is preferable.

INGREDIENTS

3 large egg whites, room temperature

¾ cup (180 ml) maple syrup

¼ teaspoon cream of tartar or lemon juice

SPECIAL EQUIPMENT

Candy thermometer

YIELD

About 5 cups (1.2 L)

METHOD

1. Combine all the ingredients in a large heatproof bowl. Place the bowl over a small or medium-sized saucepan with 2 inches (5 cm) of simmering water in it. It is important that the bottom of the bowl does not touch the water. Heat the mixture till it reaches 160°F (71°C) on a candy thermometer, whisking constantly so the eggs don't curdle or seize.

2. Remove from the heat and transfer the mixture to the bowl of a stand mixer fitted with a whisk attachment, or use a metal bowl and a hand mixer. Start whipping on low speed, gradually increasing to high over the course of 30 seconds. Continue to beat the mixture on high speed till stiff and completely cool. This could take up to 8 to 10 minutes, or longer if using a hand mixer.

Swiss Meringue Buttercream

This buttercream is light, not too sweet, and fairly easy to make, and it pipes beautifully. Because the eggs in the meringue are heated to 160°F (71°C), this is an ideal frosting for serving to kids and the elderly, as the eggs are not raw.

INGREDIENTS

1 recipe Swiss Meringue (page 57)

1½ cups (270 g) palm shortening*, room temperature

1 teaspoon vanilla extract (omit for flavor variations)

To substitute ghee, use an equal amount by weight. If measuring by volume (cups), reduce the amount of fat used to 1 cup plus 2 tablespoons.

YIELD

About 3 cups (710 ml), enough to cover and fill one 6-inch (15-cm) round, two-layer cake. This recipe doubles nicely.

METHOD

1. After making the Swiss meringue, switch to the paddle attachment on the stand mixer. (You can also use a hand mixer.) Add the shortening bit by bit, beating on medium-high speed till thick and smooth. Beat in the vanilla, if using.

2. If the buttercream becomes loose and liquid, your meringue may not have been sufficiently cool when you added the shortening. Chill the mixture slightly in the fridge, then resume beating. It will emulsify eventually. If it curdles, the shortening may have been too cold. No worries! Don't fret or throw it out; just keep beating! Beating the mixture fixes pretty much everything.

NOTE

This buttercream can be stored in a covered container in the fridge for several days or even frozen for a few months. Bring to room temperature and rewhip before using.

Flavor Variations for Swiss Meringue Buttercream:

Raspberry Meringue Buttercream

INGREDIENTS

6 ounces (170 g) raspberries, puréed and pressed through a fine-mesh sieve to remove seeds, or 3 to 4 tablespoons raspberry powder (see page 37)

1 recipe Swiss Meringue Buttercream (opposite)

Natural food coloring (optional)

METHOD

Fold 1 or 2 tablespoons of the berry puree at a time into the buttercream, till it is all incorporated. It will break and look like it has curdled, but continue mixing till it becomes smooth. It will emulsify eventually. Alternatively, you can whisk in 3 to 4 tablespoons of raspberry powder. Berry buttercreams are very light in color. If desired, you can add some natural food coloring to reach your preferred color.

Chocolate Meringue Buttercream

INGREDIENTS

3½ ounces (100 g) bittersweet chocolate or 4 to 6 tablespoons (25 to 38 g) cocoa powder, or more to taste

1 recipe Swiss Meringue Buttercream (opposite)

METHOD

If using bittersweet chocolate, melt the chocolate in a double boiler over medium-low heat, then remove from the heat and let cool to room temperature. Fold the cooled chocolate into the buttercream, mixing gently till smooth. It will break and look like it has curdled, but continue mixing till it becomes smooth. It will emulsify eventually. Alternatively, you can beat in 4 to 6 tablespoons (25 to 38 g) of cocoa powder, or more to taste.

Espresso Meringue Buttercream

INGREDIENTS

1½ tablespoons instant espresso coffee or espresso powder

1½ teaspoons boiling water

1 recipe Swiss Meringue Buttercream (opposite)

METHOD

In a small bowl, dissolve the instant espresso coffee in the boiling water. Let cool completely. Add half of the cooled espresso to the buttercream and beat till smooth. Then add more to taste.

French Buttercream

This is an intensely rich and silky buttercream due to its egg yolk base. I like to use the coffee variation in my Opera Cake recipe (page 151), but it also works beautifully for frosting cakes and piping onto cupcakes. To mix up the flavor, try replacing the vanilla with your favorite liqueurs.

INGREDIENTS

6 large egg yolks, room temperature

1 cup (240 ml) maple syrup or honey

1½ cups (270 g) palm shortening*, room temperature

1 teaspoon vanilla extract

*To substitute ghee, use an equal amount by weight. If measuring by volume (cups), reduce the amount of fat used to 1 cup plus 2 tablespoons.

SPECIAL EQUIPMENT

Candy thermometer

YIELD

About 3 cups (710 ml), enough to cover and fill one 6-inch (15-cm) round, two-layer cake

METHOD

1. Place the egg yolks in the bowl of a stand mixer fitted with a whisk attachment. Beat the yolks on high speed for about 5 minutes or till thick and light in color. While the yolks are whipping, pour the maple syrup into a saucepan and bring to a boil over medium heat. Continue to boil the syrup till it reaches a temperature of 240°F (115°C) on a candy thermometer, 12 to 15 minutes.

2. Lower the mixer speed and pour the hot syrup into the egg yolks in a slow, steady stream. Try not to hit the beaters or the syrup will splatter all over the bowl. Once all the syrup has been added, beat on high speed till the egg mixture is completely cool. This could take 8 to 10 minutes, or longer if using a hand mixer.

3. Switch to the paddle attachment and add the shortening bit by bit, beating till thick and smooth. Beat in the vanilla.

4. If the buttercream becomes loose and liquid, your egg yolks may not have been sufficiently cool when you added the shortening. Chill the mixture slightly in the fridge, then resume beating. It will emulsify eventually. If it curdles, the shortening may have been too cold. No worries! Don't fret or throw it out; just keep beating! Beating the mixture fixes pretty much everything.

VARIATION: COFFEE FRENCH BUTTERCREAM

Dissolve 2 tablespoons of instant espresso coffee or espresso powder in 2 teaspoons of boiling water. Let cool completely. While the espresso is cooling, prepare the French buttercream, then add half of the cooled espresso to the buttercream in place of the vanilla and beat till smooth. Add more to taste if desired.

Egg-Free Whipped Buttercream

This is a great alternative to the egg-based buttercreams, as it has a similar silky texture. It works nicely for frosting cakes and piping onto cupcakes. Once piped, this frosting holds up well at room temperature (75°F/24°C or less). However, it will melt (as does all buttercream) if left too long in warmer temperatures.

INGREDIENTS

1 cup (180 g) palm shortening

¾ cup (180 ml) honey or maple syrup, or more as desired

½ cup (120 ml) cold coconut cream from 1 (13½-ounce/400-ml) can full-fat coconut milk (see page 48)

¼ cup (30 g) arrowroot flour

1 tablespoon coconut flour

2 teaspoons vanilla extract

YIELD

About 2½ cups (600 ml), enough to cover and fill one 6-inch (15-cm) round, two-layer cake

METHOD

In the bowl of a stand mixer fitted with a whisk attachment, combine all the ingredients. Beat on low speed till the arrowroot flour is fully incorporated. Increase the speed to high and beat till smooth and fluffy, about 2 minutes.

Flavor Variations for Egg-Free Whipped Buttercream:

Raspberry/Strawberry Whipped Buttercream.
To the bowl with the rest of the ingredients, add ¼ cup (28 g) of freeze-dried raspberry or strawberry powder (see page 37) and beat till smooth. Add natural food coloring or more strawberry or raspberry powder to intensify the color if desired.

Coffee/Espresso Whipped Buttercream.
Omit the vanilla. To the bowl with the rest of the ingredients, add 1 tablespoon of instant espresso coffee or espresso powder and beat till smooth. Add more to taste if desired.

Maple Fondant Glaze

INGREDIENTS

1½ cups (180 g) powdered sugar (see page 33)

2 tablespoons water

1½ teaspoons maple syrup or honey

Natural colorings or flavorings of your choice (optional)

SPECIAL EQUIPMENT

Candy thermometer

YIELD

About ⅔ cup (160 ml); when doubled makes 1¼ cups (300 ml)

METHOD

1. Combine all the ingredients in a small, heavy-bottomed saucepan. Mix well and cook over very low heat till smooth and shiny. Be careful not to let the mixture exceed 100°F (38°C), or it will lose its shine. Add any colorings or flavorings you like.

2. If needed, let the glaze sit to thicken some before pouring or dipping. Any excess glaze can be stored in an airtight container in the fridge. To use, gently reheat to a pourable consistency (again, never exceeding 100°F/38°C).

NOTE

You can substitute a plain organic, grain-free powdered sugar for the powdered maple sugar. This will make colors brighter and whites pure white.

Flavor Variations for Maple Fondant Glaze:

Chocolate Fondant Glaze.
Whisk 3 to 4 tablespoons of cocoa powder into the warmed mixture. Add water by the teaspoon if needed to reach the desired consistency.

Raspberry/Strawberry Fondant Glaze.
Whisk 3 to 4 tablespoons of freeze-dried raspberry or strawberry powder (see page 37) into the warmed mixture to reach the desired flavor and color. Add water by the teaspoon if needed to reach the desired consistency.

Espresso Fondant Glaze.
Dissolve 1½ teaspoons of instant espresso coffee or espresso powder in the 2 tablespoons of water called for in the Maple Fondant Glaze recipe, then whisk to combine. Alternatively, replace half or all of the water in the recipe with freshly made espresso or strong brewed coffee.

Matcha Green Tea Fondant Glaze.
Whisk 1 to 2 tablespoons of matcha green tea powder into the warmed mixture. Add water by the teaspoon if needed to reach the desired consistency.

Lemon/Key Lime Fondant Glaze.
Replace the powdered maple sugar with a plain organic, grain-free powdered sugar and substitute lemon or Key lime juice for the water.

Vanilla Coconut Butter Glaze

This glaze is great for getting bright colors, as it does not use maple sugar. It has a softer, more matte finish than the maple sugar–based glazes, which makes it suitable for choux pastry, Bundt cakes, and donuts.

INGREDIENTS

⅓ cup (80 g) liquid coconut butter (manna)

2 tablespoons light-colored honey or maple syrup

2 tablespoons water, plus more if needed

1 teaspoon vanilla extract

YIELD

About ½ cup (120 ml)

METHOD

1. Before measuring the coconut butter, stir to fully incorporate the separated oil in the jar.

2. In a small bowl, whisk together all the ingredients till smooth and glossy. If needed, add more water by the teaspoon till the glaze reaches the desired consistency. When ready, it should look glossy and opaque and be thick enough to coat your pastry, yet thin enough that it pours right off of a spoon. If the glaze gets too liquidy, whisk in some more coconut butter.

3. To set, put the glazed pastries on a cookie sheet and place in the freezer for no more than 5 minutes. When removed from the freezer, the glaze should stay set at room temperature. It will not smudge when gently touched, but it will be soft and could easily be marked or scraped.

NOTE

For choux pastry, this glaze is best prepared just before glazing and serving. A Bundt cake or donuts can be glazed, then stored in the refrigerator.

Flavor Variations for Vanilla Coconut Butter Glaze:

Chocolate Coconut Butter Glaze.
Make the Vanilla Coconut Butter Glaze, then whisk in 1 tablespoon of cocoa powder till smooth and glossy. Add water by the teaspoon if needed to reach the desired consistency.

Espresso Coconut Butter Glaze.
Dissolve 1½ teaspoons to 1 tablespoon of instant espresso coffee or espresso powder in the 2 tablespoons of water called for in the Vanilla Coconut Butter Glaze recipe, or replace the water with freshly made espresso or strong brewed coffee. You can also replace the vanilla with coffee liqueur if you like. Add water by the teaspoon if needed to reach the desired consistency.

Tart Raspberry Coconut Butter Glaze.
Substitute lemon juice for the water called for in the Vanilla Coconut Butter Glaze recipe. Then whisk 1 tablespoon of freeze-dried raspberry powder (see page 37) into the prepared glaze till smooth and glossy. Add lemon juice by the teaspoon if needed to reach the desired consistency.

Lemon Coconut Butter Glaze.
Substitute lemon juice for the water and omit the vanilla. Whisk 1 teaspoon of grated lemon zest into the prepared glaze if desired. Add water by the teaspoon if needed to reach the desired consistency.

Ganache

Ganache is an emulsion of bittersweet chocolate and cream. It can be used as a pourable glaze or cooled and whipped up into a fluffy frosting. Some recipes in this book call for half a batch. To make half a batch, simply reduce the ingredients to ⅔ cup (160 ml) of coconut milk and 5 ounces (140 g) of chocolate.

INGREDIENTS

1¼ cups (300 ml) full-fat coconut milk

10 ounces (285 g) bittersweet chocolate chips or chopped chocolate

YIELD

1¾ cups (425 ml)

METHOD

1. Open the can of coconut milk without shaking it. Pour off the creamy part into a 2-cup (475-ml) liquid measuring cup, then add enough of the coconut water to make 1¼ cups (300 ml).

2. Place the chocolate in a heatproof bowl. In a saucepan over medium-high heat, bring the milk just to a simmer. Remove from the heat and pour the hot milk over the chocolate. Let stand for 5 minutes or till melted.

3. Using a metal spoon or small whisk, start from the center of the bowl and stir the chocolate with small circular movements, gently incorporating the milk. As the center begins to become dark and glossy, begin to make larger circular movements till the entire mixture becomes glossy and smooth.

4. To use as a glaze: Use right away, while still slightly warm. Then leave to set.

5. To use as a whipped frosting: Let cool at room temperature for at least 2 hours. Then, using a stand mixer fitted with a whisk attachment (or a hand mixer), beat till thick and fluffy. If it has trouble whipping up, chill it in the fridge for about 5 minutes and then resume whipping.

Flavor Variations for Ganache:

Mocha Ganache.
Whisk 1 tablespoon of instant espresso coffee or espresso powder into the hot milk in step 2, then continue with the recipe as directed.

Extra-Thick Ganache (for Opera Cake).
This is a thicker ganache used especially for the Opera Cake recipe on page 151. Follow the instructions above, but use just 5 ounces (140 g) of chocolate and ¼ cup (60 ml) of coconut milk.

Sweet Chocolate Glaze (Water-Based Ganache Alternative)

This glaze is often used for glazing a Sacher Torte (page 143). It also makes a great alternative to the coconut milk–based ganache and has a gorgeous sheen. It can be used for glazing éclairs, donuts, and cakes or for pouring over ice cream.

INGREDIENTS

5 ounces (140 g) bittersweet chocolate chips or finely chopped chocolate

⅓ cup (80 ml) maple syrup or honey

1 tablespoon water

1 tablespoon rum or water

YIELD

¾ cup (180 ml), enough to glaze a 6-inch (15-cm) Sacher Torte (page 143)

METHOD

1. Place the chocolate in a heatproof bowl.

2. In a saucepan, whisk together the maple syrup, water, and rum, then bring to a boil over medium-high heat. Continue to boil for about 2 minutes. Remove from the heat and pour the hot mixture over the chocolate. Let stand for 5 minutes or till melted.

3. Whisk till smooth. If the glaze is too thick to pour, whisk in up to 1 tablespoon of hot water.

4. Let cool till just warm. The glaze needs to be fluid enough to pour and cover the cake, but not so fluid that it runs right off. If it becomes too thick and starts to set, you can reheat it over a double boiler as you work.

Hard Caramel Glaze

This hard caramel is used for choux buns and Croquembouche (page 97).

INGREDIENTS

1 cup (240 ml) maple syrup or honey

1 tablespoon water

1 teaspoon lemon juice

SPECIAL EQUIPMENT

Candy thermometer

YIELD

½ cup (120 ml)

METHOD

1. Prepare an ice bath in a large bowl.

2. In a saucepan, bring all the ingredients to a boil over medium heat. Skim off any initial scum, and lower the temperature if needed to keep the mixture from boiling over. Cook without stirring till the syrup reaches about 295°F (145°C) on a candy thermometer. This will take about 25 minutes, depending on the size of the pan and the amount of heat. Caramel can burn easily toward the end of cooking, so watch it carefully.

3. When the caramel becomes quite dark and just starts to thicken a little, test it to determine whether it's ready. Dip the end of a fork in the caramel, then touch the dipped fork with a clean one and pull them apart. If the caramel is ready, it will create thin threads that turn brittle quickly as you separate the forks. When it's ready, immediately dip the bottom of the pan into the ice bath to stop the syrup from cooking.

4. Use immediately. The caramel can be gently reheated up to two times if needed. After that it will start to crystallize. Do not stir the caramel while reheating it, or it will begin to crystallize.

Praline Paste

This delicious candy is made with toasted hazelnuts that are then puréed into a sweet nut butter. It is used to flavor pastry creams and more.

INGREDIENTS

1½ cups (230 g) raw hazelnuts

1 recipe Hard Caramel Glaze (opposite)

YIELD

⅔ cup (160 ml)

METHOD

1. Preheat the oven to 350°F (177°C). Place the hazelnuts on a rimmed baking sheet and bake for about 12 minutes, till the skins start to loosen. Transfer to a flour sack towel and rub the nuts till much of the skins are removed. (It's okay if not all of them come off.) Roughly chop the nuts and place them on a large sheet of parchment paper.

2. Make the caramel glaze according to the instructions, but skip the ice bath part. When it reaches temperature, pour the caramel evenly over the nuts. Place in the freezer for 5 to 8 minutes or till hardened.

3. Chop into small pieces and purée with a food processor or high-powered blender till smooth.

fondant

bun

filling

Chapter 3:

CHOUX PASTRY

For me, choux pastries have always been a means of expressing some of life's deeper, more meaningful sentiments. Éclairs, profiteroles, cream puffs—these are the things that I make for people when I truly want them to understand what they mean to me. They are romance; they are intimacy. They are symbols of genuine friendship and are one of my favorite ways to show my affection to those I hold dear.

ABOUT PÂTE À CHOUX

Pâte à choux is a light and crispy pastry typically used for éclairs, cream puffs, beignets, and more. Choux pastry is made simply with flour, eggs, water or milk, and a fat. It is cooked on the stovetop, then piped and baked at high heat. The heat and liquid in the recipe work together to create steam, causing the dough to puff up as it cooks.

This chapter includes a number of different recipes ranging from classic standards to my own creative interpretations. Ultimately, these recipes are intended to serve as examples to inspire your own creativity.

TIPS FOR MAKING
AND SERVING BEAUTIFUL CHOUX

If your parchment paper curls when you are lining your pan, grease the entire cookie sheet and then press the parchment paper onto it. Smooth out any major wrinkles, as they can make the choux pastry spread unevenly while baking. Or use reusable parchment paper, which naturally lies flatter.

To produce consistently sized éclairs or buns, it helps to draw guidelines on the underside of the parchment paper. See pages 266–267 for an illustrated example.

When piping the dough, use smooth upward movements as you squeeze. When finishing each bun or éclair shell, release pressure and pause for a moment before lifting the tip away.

Piped, unbaked pastry shells can be frozen till hard and then stored in a freezer bag for easy access. You can bake them straight from the freezer—no thawing required. Simply brush on an egg wash and bake as instructed.

The pastries in this chapter are best served within an hour of assembly, as choux pastry shells and buns become soggy once filled.

Pâte à Choux

See photo instructions on pages 264–265.

INGREDIENTS

1 cup (120 g) arrowroot flour

2 tablespoons coconut flour

1 teaspoon maple sugar

Pinch of salt

⅓ cup (65 g) palm shortening

½ cup (120 ml) full-fat coconut milk

¼ cup (60 ml) water

4 large eggs, room temperature

1 large egg plus 1 tablespoon water, for the egg wash

YIELD

25 petite buns, 8 large buns, 15 petite éclairs, or 8 large éclairs

METHOD

1. Preheat the oven to 400°F (205°C) and grease and line a large cookie sheet with parchment paper.

2. In a medium-sized bowl, whisk together the flours, sugar, and salt. In a small saucepan over medium heat, combine the shortening, coconut milk, and water. Once the shortening has melted, continue to heat the mixture till a few bubbles just break the surface. Do not let it boil. *This step will determine how many eggs you will end up needing later, as the heat of the mixture will affect the absorption rate of the arrowroot and the evaporation of the water. You may need more or less egg in the final phase to get the desired consistency of dough.*

3. Remove from the heat and pour the flour mixture into the hot milk mixture. Immediately stir, slowly at first to incorporate the flour, then vigorously till the mixture forms a big, soft blob of dough. Transfer the dough to a stand mixer fitted with a paddle attachment. Stir on low speed for about a minute to cool it down. While the mixture is cooling, beat one of the eggs in a small bowl and set aside.

4. Turn the mixer up to medium speed and add one egg at a time to the dough, beating each egg before adding it. Allow each egg to be completely incorporated before adding the next, as the dough will break or separate with each addition. After adding the first three eggs, increase the mixer speed and beat for about a minute or till the dough smooths out. Add more beaten egg a little at a time till the dough is creamy looking and reaches the desired consistency. To determine the ideal consistency, take a little dough between your index finger and thumb. You should be able to pull it into soft, sticky threads. The best way I can describe the texture is that it should be like chewing gum on a hot sidewalk.

5. Pipe and bake the dough following the instructions on pages 76–77.

Flavor Variations for Pâte à Choux:

Coconut-Free Pâte à Choux.
Prepare the dough according to the recipe, but replace the 2 tablespoons of coconut flour with ¼ cup (30 g) of almond flour and replace the coconut milk and water with ¾ cup (185 ml) of the nondairy milk of your choice.

Chocolate Pâte à Choux (nut-free).
Prepare the dough according to the recipe, but replace the 2 tablespoons of coconut flour with 3 tablespoons of cocoa powder.

SIZING AND PIPING

Petite Choux Buns: These round buns are perfect for making small cream puffs or appetizers.

Using a mini (1¼-inch/3-cm) mechanical scoop, scoop out approximately 25 level mounds of the pâte à choux onto the prepared baking sheet, spacing them about 1 inch (2.5 cm) apart. Alternatively, you can transfer the dough to a large pastry bag fitted with a ½-inch (1.25-cm) round tip and pipe 1½-inch (4-cm) rounds.

Large Choux Buns: These round buns are perfect for making large cream puffs, profiteroles, or sandwich buns.

Using a medium-sized (2-inch/5-cm) mechanical scoop, scoop out approximately 8 level mounds of the pâte à choux onto the prepared baking sheet, spacing them about 2 inches (5 cm) apart. Alternatively, you can use a ¼-cup (60-ml) measuring cup to portion out the dough.

Petite and Large Éclair Shells: These oblong shells are perfect for making éclairs.

Using a large pastry bag fitted with a ½-inch (1.25-cm) plain tip, pipe the pâte à choux into approximately fifteen 3½-inch (9-cm)-long, 1-inch (2.5-cm)-wide logs for small éclairs or eight 5-inch (12.75-cm)-long, 1-inch (2.5-cm)-wide logs for large éclairs. Space them about 2 inches (5 cm) apart on the prepared baking sheet.

BAKING

All the pastry shells in this section are baked starting at 400°F (205°C). Baking times will vary depending on the size of the pastry and are listed below. Bake on the center rack of the oven.

1. Prepare an egg wash by whisking together 1 large egg and 1 tablespoon of water. Using a pastry brush or your fingers, gently coat the piped dough with a thin layer of egg wash.

2. **For petite buns and éclair shells:** Bake for 15 minutes, then lower the oven temperature to 350°F (177°C) and bake for approximately 10 to 12 more minutes, till puffed, golden, and firm to the touch.

3. **For large buns and éclair shells:** Bake for 15 minutes, then lower the oven temperature to 350°F (177°C) and bake for approximately 20 to 25 more minutes, till puffed, golden, and firm to the touch.

4. Remove from the oven and transfer to a wire rack to cool.

NOTE

If you're not sure whether the choux pastries are done, simply remove one from the oven and set it on a wire rack for a minute. If it begins to soften and/or sink in, give the pastries about 5 more minutes in the oven.

LARGE ÉCLAIR
5 inches (12.5 cm) long

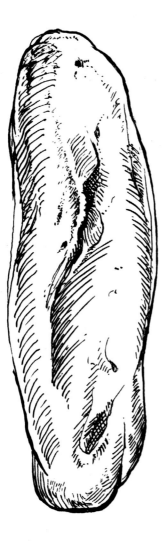

LARGE BUN
3 inches (7.5 cm) round

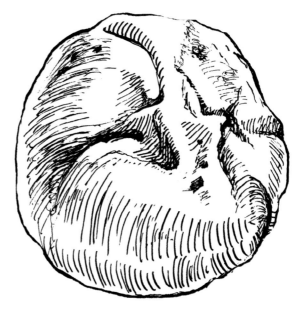

PETITE ÉCLAIR
3½ inches (9 cm) long

PETITE BUN
2 inches (5 cm) round

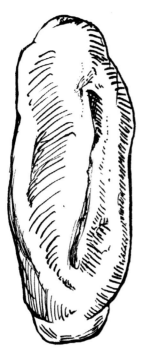

Blackberry Almond Crusted Éclairs

INGREDIENTS

1 large egg plus 1 tablespoon water, for the egg wash

1 recipe Petite Éclair Shells (page 76)

1 cup (90 g) sliced almonds

1 recipe Blackberry Jam (page 51) or 1 cup (240 ml) store-bought

¼ cup (30 g) powdered sugar* (see page 33; optional)

Regular powdered sugar can be substituted for maple powdered sugar if a white dusting is preferred.

YIELD

15 petite éclairs

METHOD

1. When ready to assemble the éclairs, preheat the oven to 350°F (177°C) and line a large cookie sheet with parchment paper.

2. Beat the egg and water together in a small bowl. Using a pastry brush or your fingers, lightly coat the top of each pastry shell with the egg wash. Press the sliced almonds all over the tops of the shells. Place the shells on the prepared cookie sheet and bake for 5 minutes or till the egg wash is dry and the almonds are secure. Let cool on a wire rack.

3. Carefully slice each shell in half lengthwise and remove the top. Try to keep each top piece matched up with its bottom piece so they fit together later.

4. Soften the jam by beating it with a spoon. Using the spoon, distribute the filling evenly among the open shells. Place the tops back on, then dust with powdered sugar if desired.

Candied Banana Éclairs

INGREDIENTS

1 recipe Large Éclair Shells (page 76)

1 recipe Banana Pastry Cream (page 46)

1 recipe Sweetened Whipped Cream (page 48)

½ recipe Ganache (page 66)

For the candied bananas:

3 small bananas

⅓ cup (70 g) firmly packed maple sugar

1 (3-ounce/85-g) bar bittersweet chocolate, finely shaved, for garnish

SPECIAL EQUIPMENT

Pastry bag fitted with a ½-inch (1.25-cm) French tip

Kitchen torch

YIELD

8 large éclairs

METHOD

1. When ready to assemble the éclairs, slice the pastry shells in half lengthwise and remove the tops. Try to keep each top piece matched up with its bottom piece so they fit together later.

2. Using the pastry bag or a spoon, divide the pastry cream evenly among the open pastry shells, approximately 2 tablespoons per shell. Then, using the pastry bag, pipe the whipped cream on top of the pastry cream in a decorative manner. One at a time, dip each pastry shell top in the ganache and place on top of a filled shell.

3. Make the candied bananas (see pages 268–269 for photo instructions): Slice the bananas lengthwise into ⅛-inch (3-mm) strips. Lay them out on a sheet of parchment paper and sprinkle generously with the sugar. Use a kitchen torch to caramelize the top of each banana.

4. Carefully place a banana slice on top of each éclair. Sprinkle with the shaved chocolate.

Passion Fruit Meringue Éclairs

INGREDIENTS

1 recipe Large Éclair Shells
(page 76)

1 recipe Passion Fruit Curd
(page 52)

1 large egg white

¼ cup (60 ml) maple syrup or
honey

⅛ teaspoon cream of tartar
(optional)

SPECIAL EQUIPMENT

*Pastry bag fitted with a ½-inch
(1.25-cm) French or star tip*

Kitchen torch (optional)

YIELD

8 large éclairs

METHOD

1. When ready to assemble the éclairs, slice the pastry shells in half lengthwise and remove the tops. Try to keep each top piece matched up with its bottom piece so they fit together later.

2. Using a spoon, divide the curd evenly among the open pastry shells. Place the tops back on.

3. Use the egg white, maple syrup, and cream of tartar to make a small batch of Swiss meringue following the instructions on page 57. Transfer to the pastry bag and pipe the meringue on top of each éclair in a decorative pattern. Once all the éclairs have been topped with meringue, use a small kitchen torch to caramelize the meringue on each éclair, if desired.

Matcha Green Tea Cream Puffs with Ganache

INGREDIENTS

1 recipe Petite Choux Buns
(page 76)

1 recipe Matcha Green Tea
Pastry Cream (page 47)

½ recipe Ganache (page 66)

SPECIAL EQUIPMENT

*Pastry bag fitted with a ½-inch
(1.25-cm) French or star tip
(optional)*

YIELD

25 small cream puffs

METHOD

1. When ready to assemble the cream puffs, slice the choux buns in half. Try to keep each top piece with its bottom piece so they match up later.

2. Using the pastry bag or a spoon, fill the open buns generously with the pastry cream.

3. One at a time, dip each top piece in the ganache and place on top of a filled bun. Alternatively, drizzle the ganache over the tops of the assembled cream puffs.

Peaches and Caramel Topped Cream Puffs

INGREDIENTS

1 recipe Large Choux Buns
(page 76)

1 recipe Hard Caramel Glaze
(page 68)

Double recipe Sweetened
Whipped Cream (page 48)

1 to 2 fresh peaches

Lemon juice, for coating the
peach slices (optional)

Double recipe Pastry Cream
(page 46)

SPECIAL EQUIPMENT

*Pastry bag fitted with a ½-inch
(1.25-cm) French or star tip
(optional)*

YIELD

8 cream puffs

METHOD

1. When ready to assemble the cream puffs, line a large cookie sheet with parchment paper. Slice the choux buns in half. Try to keep each top piece with its bottom piece so they match up later.

2. Prepare the caramel glaze. Immediately dip the top of each bun into the glaze and place caramel side up on the prepared cookie sheet. Let cool till hard and set.

3. When ready to serve, prepare the whipped cream and thinly slice the peaches. If desired, coat the peaches in lemon juice to keep them from browning. Using a spoon, divide the pastry cream among the open choux buns, about ¼ cup per bun, then scoop or decoratively pipe each bun with a generous amount of whipped cream. Place a caramel-glazed top on each filled bun and serve.

Espresso Cream Filled Éclairs with Candied Bacon

INGREDIENTS

For the candied bacon:

8 slices bacon

⅔ cup (160 ml) maple syrup

1 recipe Petite Éclair Shells (page 76)

1 recipe Espresso Whipped Cream (page 49)

1 recipe Espresso Fondant Glaze (page 63), or more if needed

SPECIAL EQUIPMENT

Pastry bag fitted with a bismarck tip

YIELD

15 petite éclairs

METHOD

1. Make the candied bacon: Preheat the oven to 400°F (200°C). Arrange the bacon in a 9 by 13-inch (23 by 33-cm) baking dish or a rimmed baking sheet lined with parchment paper. Bake for 15 minutes, then remove from the oven and carefully pour off the fat. Reduce the oven temperature to 350°F (177°C).

2. Cut each slice of bacon in half, making 16 pieces. Generously brush the bacon with the maple syrup, flip it over, and coat the other side. Return it to the oven and bake for another 15 minutes, then flip the bacon again and rotate the pan. Return it to the oven once more and bake till the bacon is golden and the syrup is thick, 10 to 15 minutes. Watch closely in the last 5 minutes to prevent burning. Remove from the oven, transfer to a clean sheet of parchment paper, and let cool. The bacon should become crunchy as it cools.

3. When ready to assemble the éclairs, use a skewer to poke a hole in either end of each shell. Using the pastry bag, pipe the whipped cream into the shells from both sides.

4. Prepare the glaze. Dip the top of each éclair into the glaze, then hold it vertically over the bowl, letting the excess drip off. Be sure the glaze covers the holes. Place a whole piece of candied bacon on top of each éclair and leave to set.

NOTE

Make extra glaze if needed. The amount needed can vary depending on how thick you make the glaze.

Double Chocolate Blackberry Cream Puffs

INGREDIENTS

1 recipe Large Chocolate Choux Buns (page 76)

Double recipe Chocolate Whipped Cream (page 49)

2 cups (12 ounces/340 g) fresh blackberries

¼ cup (30 g) powdered sugar (see page 33; optional)

SPECIAL EQUIPMENT

Pastry bag fitted with a ½-inch (1.25-cm) French or star tip

8 toothpicks

YIELD

8 cream puffs

METHOD

1. When ready to assemble the cream puffs, slice the choux buns in half. Try to keep each top piece with its bottom piece so they match up later.

2. Divide the blackberries evenly among the open buns, reserving 8 berries for garnish.

3. Using the pastry bag, pipe a generous amount of whipped cream on top of the blackberries in each bun, then place the top piece on each of the filled buns.

4. To garnish, secure a blackberry to the top of each cream puff using a toothpick.

5. If desired, lightly dust the cream puffs with powdered sugar.

Croquembouche

This traditional French dessert consists of choux buns filled with pastry cream. After being filled, the buns are piled into a cone shape and "glued" together with a hard caramel. This is an elaborate undertaking that takes a fair amount of skill to accomplish. (See the photo instructions on pages 270–271.) It must be served within hours of assembly or it will become soft and fall apart.

INGREDIENTS

Double recipe (about 50) Petite Choux Buns (page 76)

Double recipe Pastry Cream (page 46)

2 batches Hard Caramel Glaze (page 68)

Coarse sugar, for decorating (optional)

SPECIAL EQUIPMENT

18-inch (46-cm) foam floral cone

Pastry bag fitted with a bismarck tip

SERVES

About 12

METHOD

1. Cover the foam floral cone with parchment paper and place it upright on an additional sheet of parchment.

2. Use a skewer to poke a hole in the bottom of each choux bun. Using the pastry bag, pipe the pastry cream into each bun through the hole.

3. Prepare one batch of the caramel glaze. Dip the top of each bun into the caramel, then dip half of them in the coarse sugar, if using. Place them caramel side up on a sheet of parchment paper and leave to harden.

4. Prepare the second batch of caramel glaze. Dip the side of one bun into the caramel and stick another bun to it. Place at the base of the cone with the hardened caramel facing outward. Repeat with additional buns, placing the buns dipped in coarse sugar (if using) at random, wrapping them closely around the cone till the base layer has been completed. Repeat this process, adding tiers. Offset the buns using caramel everywhere they touch each other till you've used all the buns or you've reached the top of the cone. Make sure that the buns are being glued to each other and not to the parchment-covered mold. Leave the assembled croquembouche in place till the caramel is hard and set.

5. Carefully unmold the croquembouche by lifting it off the parchment paper, putting as little inward pressure on it as possible, as it can be fragile. Set on a nonslippery serving base.

6. Keep in a cool, dry place for no longer than 4 hours before serving. Do not store in the refrigerator or the caramel will become sticky and soft.

Praline Paris Brest

This is a delicious French dessert consisting of a large baked ring of choux pastry filled with praline pastry cream. (See pages 272–273 for photo instructions.) It can be filled simply with sweetened whipped cream and fruit as well.

The pastry cream needs to be made a few hours to a day in advance so that it is completely chilled and set before you proceed with the recipe.

INGREDIENTS

1 recipe Pâte à Choux (page 74)

1 large egg plus 1 tablespoon water, for the egg wash

¼ cup (25 g) sliced almonds

For the pastry cream:

1 recipe Praline Pastry Cream (page 47), well chilled

½ cup (120 g) ghee, room temperature

Double recipe Sweetened Whipped Cream (page 48)

½ cup (3 ounces/85 g) fresh raspberries

Powdered sugar (see page 33), for dusting (optional)

SPECIAL EQUIPMENT

Pastry bag fitted with a ½-inch (1.25-cm) round tip

Pastry bag fitted with a ½-inch (1.25-cm) star or French tip

SERVES

8

METHOD

1. Preheat the oven to 400°F (205°C). Draw an 8-inch (20-cm) circle on a sheet of parchment paper. I like to use a cake pan for this, but anything 8 inches (20 cm) in diameter will work. Flip the parchment over and place it on a cookie sheet.

2. Using the pastry bag with the round tip, pipe a circle of dough around the guide. Pipe another circle inside the first one, making sure they are touching. Finally, pipe one more circle on top of the two circles.

3. Make an egg wash by beating together the egg and water. Coat the whole ring with the egg wash and sprinkle with the almonds. Bake on the lower rack of the oven for 15 minutes. Move to the middle rack, then turn the oven temperature down to 350°F (177°C) and bake for another 20 minutes or till golden and crisp. Remove from the oven and let cool on a wire rack.

4. Using a large serrated knife, slice the ring in half horizontally to create two thin rings.

5. Prepare the pastry cream: In a large bowl or the bowl of a stand mixer fitted with a whisk attachment, beat the chilled praline pastry cream till smooth, then add 1 tablespoon of ghee at a time and continue beating till smooth and fluffy. If it is too soft to pipe, refrigerate for about 10 minutes, but not so long that it hardens.

6. Using the pastry bag with the star or French tip, pipe the pastry cream decoratively into the bottom half of the pastry ring. Then, using a clean bag and the same tip, pipe the whipped cream on top. Place the raspberries in a ring on top of the whipped cream, then place the second pastry ring on top. Dust with powdered sugar, if desired, and serve right away.

BUILD YOUR OWN CHOUX

PICK A CHOUX PASTRY
(pages 74–75)

☐ Pâte à Choux

☐ Chocolate Pâte à Choux

PICK A SHAPE AND SIZE
(pages 76–77)

☐ Petite Choux Buns

☐ Large Choux Buns

☐ Petite Éclair Shells

☐ Large Éclair Shells

PICK A FILLING

Note: Large buns and large éclair shells need double recipes of filling.

Pastry Creams (pages 46–47)

☐ Pastry Cream

☐ Banana Pastry Cream

☐ Matcha Green Tea Pastry Cream

☐ Pistachio Pastry Cream

☐ Praline Pastry Cream

Whipped Creams (pages 48–49)

☐ Sweetened Whipped Cream

☐ Chocolate Whipped Cream

☐ Raspberry Whipped Cream

☐ Matcha Green Tea Whipped Cream

☐ Espresso Whipped Cream

Jams (pages 50–51)

☐ Orange Marmalade

☐ Apricot Jam

☐ Blackberry Jam

☐ Raspberry Jam

Curds (page 52)

☐ Lemon Curd

☐ Passion Fruit Curd

Other Fillings

☐ Zabaglione (page 53)

☐ Whipped Ganache (page 66)

PICK A GLAZE OR TOPPING

Glazes (pages 62–67)

☐ Maple Fondant Glaze

☐ Chocolate Fondant Glaze

☐ Raspberry Fondant Glaze

☐ Espresso Fondant Glaze

☐ Matcha Green Tea Fondant Glaze

☐ Lemon Fondant Glaze

☐ Key Lime Fondant Glaze

☐ Vanilla Coconut Butter Glaze

☐ Chocolate Coconut Butter Glaze

☐ Espresso Coconut Butter Glaze

☐ Tart Raspberry Coconut Butter Glaze

☐ Lemon Coconut Butter Glaze

☐ Ganache

☐ Sweet Chocolate Glaze

Other Topping

☐ Swiss Meringue (page 57)

PICK A GARNISH

☐ Candied bananas (page 84)

☐ Candied bacon (page 93)

☐ Whatever your creativity inspires

topping

crust

filling

Chapter 4:

TARTS

Tarts are among the most elegant, rustic, and charming parts of traditional pastry making. They combine the sophistication and refinement of the big city with the charm and nostalgia of the countryside.

When dreaming up tart combinations, I've found that it's all too easy to get sidetracked by the many amazing options for fillings and toppings—to the point that one can almost entirely overlook the importance that the crust plays in making a truly great tart.

ABOUT TARTS

A tart is a baked dish consisting of a filling over a crust with an open, uncovered top. The filling can be sweet or savory. A tartlet is a miniature tart, typically around 2 inches (5 cm) in diameter.

The crust is the foundation of a tart. It adds flavor, texture, and beauty and ultimately can make or break the tart, no matter how wonderful the filling. Because grain-free flours can have stronger flavors, I prefer to make my crusts on the thinner side, around ⅛ inch (3 mm) thick. This helps to prevent the flavor of the crust from competing with the filling. Making great tarts begins with making great crusts, so that's where we're going to start.

SHAPING AND CHILLING DOUGH

For the shortbread and chocolate crust recipes (see pages 274–275 for photo instructions):

For 9-, 4-, and 3-inch (23-, 10-, and 7.5-cm) pans: You will get the best results by rolling out the chilled dough between two sheets of parchment paper into a ⅛-inch (3-mm)-thick round. I recommend using rolling pin guide rings (see page 42) to get the perfect thickness. Chill the rolled-out dough on a cookie sheet in the freezer for 5 minutes or till the top sheet of parchment paper peels off easily. Do not chill it for too long, though, as you want the dough to be flexible enough to be shaped into the pans.

Gently flip the dough over one large tart pan or a few smaller ones set close together. Carefully peel off the second sheet of parchment paper and use your fingers to maneuver and press the dough into the pan(s). Use pieces of excess dough to finish off the edges or fill in cracks and tears. If you're using 3- or 4-inch (7.5- or 10-cm) pans, you may want to do just a few at a time, rerolling the dough as needed.

For a mini tart pan or individual 2-inch (5-cm) pans: It's easiest to work a portion of dough manually into each pan to a thickness of about ⅛ inch (3 mm).

Prick the dough all over with a fork, then chill in the freezer for 10 minutes. Follow the individual baking times and unmolding instructions in the recipes found in this chapter.

Note: Alternatively, you can skip the rolling and just work the dough evenly into the pan. However, rolling the dough will give the most uniform results.

For the macaroon and coconut flour crust recipes:

Divide the dough into equal portions if needed, and then simply press the dough evenly into the pan(s) to a thickness of about ⅛ inch (3 mm). The coconut flour crust will need to be pricked all over and chilled in the same way as the almond flour–based crusts. The macaroon crusts do not require chilling and can go straight into the oven. Follow the individual baking times and unmolding instructions in the recipes found in this chapter.

Shortbread Crust

A sturdy, sweet shortbread crust made with almond flour.

INGREDIENTS

1½ cups (160 g) almond flour

2 tablespoons arrowroot flour

Pinch of salt

3 tablespoons maple syrup or honey

3 tablespoons palm shortening or ghee, softened

2 teaspoons vanilla extract

YIELD

One 9-inch (23-cm) crust, four 4-inch (10-cm) crusts, five or six 3-inch (7.5-cm) crusts, or 12 mini crusts using a 12-well mini tart pan

METHOD

1. Preheat the oven to 325°F (163°C).

2. In a large bowl, whisk together the flours and salt till blended. Add the remaining ingredients and mix till a soft dough has formed. Gather up the dough, wrap in plastic, and chill for about 15 minutes or till firm enough to be rolled out.

3. Shape into the desired pan(s) according to the "Shaping and Chilling Dough" instructions on page 105.

4. Bake for the following times or till golden all over:

mini (2 inches/5 cm), 15 to 18 minutes

small (3 inches/7.5 cm), 18 to 20 minutes

medium (4 inches/10 cm), 20 to 22 minutes

large (9 inches/23 cm), 22 to 25 minutes

Times can vary according to the thickness of the dough. For best results, rotate the pan(s) halfway through baking.

5. Remove from the oven, let cool in the pan(s), and then gently remove from the pan(s). A larger crust can remain in the pan till filled and/or served, to protect the crust from breaking.

Chocolate Crust

A delicious chocolaty crust made with almond flour.

INGREDIENTS

1¼ cups (130 g) almond flour

⅓ cup (35 g) cocoa powder

3 tablespoons maple sugar

Pinch of salt

¼ cup (45 g) palm shortening or ghee, softened

1 large egg yolk

1 tablespoon cold water

1 teaspoon vanilla extract

YIELD

One 9-inch (23-cm) crust, four 4-inch (10-cm) crusts, five or six 3-inch (7.5-cm) crusts, or 12 mini crusts using a 12-well mini tart pan

METHOD

1. Preheat the oven to 325°F (163°C).

2. In a large bowl, whisk together the flour, cocoa, sugar, and salt till blended. Add the remaining ingredients and mix till a soft dough has formed. Gather up the dough, wrap in plastic, and chill for about 10 minutes or till firm enough to be rolled out.

3. Shape into the desired pan(s) according to the "Shaping and Chilling Dough" instructions on page 105.

4. Bake for the following times or till golden all over:

   mini (2 inches/5 cm), 15 to 18 minutes

   small (3 inches/7.5 cm), 18 to 20 minutes

   medium (4 inches/10 cm), 20 to 22 minutes

   large (9 inches/23 cm), 22 to 25 minutes

Times can vary according to the thickness of the dough. For best results, rotate the pan(s) halfway through baking.

5. Remove from the oven, let cool in the pan(s), and then gently remove from the pan(s). A larger crust can remain in the pan till filled and/or served, to protect the crust from breaking.

Nut-Free Sweet Crust

This is a very delicate crust made with coconut flour. It can be used in place of any of the sweet or shortbread crusts found in this book, but it works best when it is precooked and then filled.

INGREDIENTS

½ cup (60 g) coconut flour

⅓ cup (40 g) arrowroot flour

Pinch of salt

½ cup (90 g) palm shortening or ghee, softened

2 large eggs, cold

1 tablespoon maple sugar

Cold water as needed

YIELD

One 9-inch (23-cm) crust, four 4-inch (10-cm) crusts, five or six 3-inch (7.5-cm) crusts, or 12 mini crusts using a 12-well mini tart pan

METHOD

1. Preheat the oven to 325°F (163°C).

2. In a large bowl, whisk together the flours and salt till blended. Add the remaining ingredients and mix with a wooden spoon till a soft, wet dough has formed. Gather up the dough, wrap in plastic, and chill for about 10 minutes.

3. Press the dough evenly into the desired pan(s) to a thickness of about ⅛ inch (3 mm). If using several smaller pans, divide the dough into equal portions first.

4. Prick all over with a fork and chill in the freezer for about 10 minutes.

5. Bake for the following times or till golden all over:

   mini (2 inches/5 cm), 15 to 18 minutes

   small (3 inches/7.5 cm), 18 to 20 minutes

   medium (4 inches/10 cm), 20 to 22 minutes

   large (9 inches/23 cm), 22 to 25 minutes

Times can vary according to the thickness of the dough. For best results, rotate the pan(s) halfway through baking.

6. Remove from the oven, let cool in the pan(s), and then gently remove from the pan(s). A larger crust can remain in the pan till filled and/or served, to protect the crust from breaking.

Macaroon Crust

This incredibly versatile crust is simple to make, delicious, and naturally egg-free. It can be used for any of the tart recipes that call for precooked fillings for a great egg-free and nut-free alternative.

INGREDIENTS

2 cups (160 g) unsweetened shredded coconut

¼ cup (55 g) coconut oil, softened

3 tablespoons honey

1 tablespoon full-fat coconut milk or other milk

1 teaspoon vanilla extract

Pinch of salt

YIELD

One 9-inch (23-cm) crust, four 4-inch (10-cm) crusts, five or six 3-inch (7.5-cm) crusts, or 12 mini crusts using a 12-well mini tart pan

METHOD

1. Preheat the oven to 325°F (163°C).

2. In a medium-sized bowl, mix together all the ingredients till well combined. The dough should clump together when squeezed in your hand. Because the size of coconut shreds varies, you may need to adjust the amount of liquid or shredded coconut to get the desired consistency. In this case, it is not a science.

3. Press the dough evenly into the desired pan(s) to a thickness of about ⅛ inch (3 mm). If using several smaller pans, divide the dough into equal portions first. For larger macaroon crusts, it is helpful to put foil or a silicone crust protector on the rim to keep the sides from burning.

4. Bake for the following times or till golden all over:

   mini (2 inches/5 cm), 15 to 18 minutes

   small (3 inches/7.5 cm), 18 to 20 minutes

   medium (4 inches/10 cm), 20 to 22 minutes

   large (9 inches/23 cm), 22 to 25 minutes

Times can vary according to the thickness of the dough. For best results, rotate the pan(s) halfway through baking.

5. Let cool completely before removing from the pan(s) and filling, as these crusts are fragile when warm.

VARIATION: CHOCOLATE MACAROON CRUST

Use only 1¾ cups (140 g) of shredded coconut and add 3 tablespoons of cocoa powder.

French Apple Tart

INGREDIENTS

1 recipe Shortbread Crust dough (page 106)

For the filling:

6 large Granny Smith apples (2 lbs/900 g)

3 tablespoons palm shortening or ghee

4 tablespoons (60 ml) maple syrup or honey

1 teaspoon grated lemon zest (about 1 lemon)

½ teaspoon ground cinnamon

SPECIAL EQUIPMENT

9-inch (23-cm) round tart pan with removable base

YIELD

One 9-inch (23-cm) tart (serving 6 to 8)

METHOD

1. Preheat the oven to 325°F (163°C).

2. Chill and shape the dough in the tart pan according to the instructions on page 105. Once chilled, place the crust in the oven and par-bake for 10 minutes or till just dry to the touch but not browned. Remove from the oven (but keep the oven on) and set aside to cool.

3. Make the filling: Peel, slice, and core three of the apples. Uniformity is not necessary with this batch. In a large skillet, melt 1 tablespoon of the shortening with 2 tablespoons of the maple syrup, the lemon zest, and ¼ teaspoon of the cinnamon. Add the apple slices and cook over medium heat for about 7 minutes, stirring occasionally. Once they are soft, gently mash the apples with the back of a spoon and continue to cook till most of the liquid evaporates.

4. Peel, core, and cut the rest of the apples into even ¼-inch (6-mm)-thick slices. These will garnish the top of the tart, so uniformity is helpful here. Melt 1 tablespoon of the shortening with the remaining 2 tablespoons of maple syrup and remaining ¼ teaspoon of cinnamon. Add the apples and cook for about 5 minutes or till they just begin to soften. Set aside to cool in their syrup.

5. Spoon the mashed filling into the cooled crust. Arrange the apple slices in concentric, overlapping circles over the filling. Melt the remaining tablespoon of shortening and brush the tops of the apples with it.

6. Bake for 25 minutes. To prevent the sides of the crust from burning, you can take a piece of parchment paper and cut out a circle slightly smaller than 9 inches (23 cm) in the center of the rectangle. Place the rectangle over the tart so that the edges are covered but the center is exposed.

7. The tart can be covered and stored in the fridge for up to 2 days.

Citron Tart

This classic French tart can be found at patisseries and cafés year-round. It is especially delicious topped with Sweetened Whipped Cream (page 48).

INGREDIENTS

1 (9-inch/23-cm) Shortbread Crust (page 106), prebaked

1 recipe Lemon Curd (page 52)

1 (3-ounce/85-g) bar bittersweet chocolate (optional)

SPECIAL EQUIPMENT

9-inch (23-cm) round tart pan with removable base

Small pastry bag fitted with a small, plain, round tip (optional)

YIELD

One 9-inch (23-cm) tart (serving 6 to 8)

METHOD

1. Preheat the oven to 325°F (163°C).

2. Prepare the lemon curd and, while it is still warm, strain it directly into the cooled crust. Spread out the curd with a spoon or gently tilt the pan from side to side. This will form a thin layer of curd and make for a tall-looking crust.

3. Place the tart in the oven for 5 minutes to set the curd. Remove from the oven and let cool to room temperature.

4. If desired, and if you are adventurous, write "Citron" over the curd with melted chocolate. To do so, melt the chocolate over gentle heat, let it cool slightly to thicken up some, and then scoop the chocolate into the pastry bag and go for it.

5. This tart is best eaten the day it is made but can be stored, covered, in the fridge for 1 to 2 days. The crust will soften over time.

No-Crust Black-Bottomed Banana Pies

Making no-crust pies is a great and easy option for serving tart-style desserts in a fun new way, or for serving them to people whose dietary restrictions don't allow for any kind of crust. Be creative; the possibilities are endless.

INGREDIENTS

1 recipe Ganache (page 66)

1 to 2 bananas

1 recipe Pastry Cream (page 46)

1 recipe Swiss Meringue (page 57)

SPECIAL EQUIPMENT

4 (8-ounce/240-ml) parfait-style cups

Kitchen torch (optional)

SERVES

4

METHOD

1. When ready to assemble the pies, prepare the ganache, then pour about ¼ cup (60 ml) into each cup. Chill for 15 minutes or till the ganache is cool. Otherwise, it will melt the pastry cream.

2. Once the ganache has set, slice the bananas into ¼-inch (6-mm) rounds. Lay them in an even layer over the ganache, then put about ¼ cup (60 ml) of the pastry cream on top of the bananas. Cover and chill the cups till ready to serve.

3. Just before serving, make the Swiss meringue and pipe or pile it nice and high on top of the cream filling. If desired, use a kitchen torch to brown the meringue topping. Either serve right away or chill and serve within 2 hours, or the meringue will begin to weep and break down.

Mixed Berry Tarts

The classic berry tart is a staple found in pastry shops everywhere. With its fresh, slightly sweet attributes, it's always a crowd-pleaser. This tart would also be delicious with the Macaroon Crust (page 109) for a nut-free variation.

INGREDIENTS

1 cup (170 g) fresh blackberries

1 cup (170 g) fresh raspberries

1 cup (170 g) fresh blueberries

1 recipe Pastry Cream (page 46)

5 (3-inch/7.5-cm) Shortbread Crusts (page 106), prebaked

YIELD

Five 3-inch (7.5-cm) tarts

METHOD

1. When ready to assemble the tarts, combine the berries in a large bowl and gently mix them together. Divide the pastry cream evenly among the crusts. They don't need to be overly full, as the berries will sink into the cream and cause it to rise up. Pile the berries on top of the tarts.

2. These tarts are best assembled and served right away. They can be chilled for a few hours, but eventually the crusts will begin to absorb moisture and lose their crispness.

Frangipane Pear Tarts with Chocolate Crust

Frangipane is simply a filling made from almonds. This tart is a standard in many French-style pastry shops. I've given it a little twist by pairing the filling with a chocolate crust.

INGREDIENTS

1 recipe Chocolate Crust dough (page 107)

For the frangipane:

½ cup (90 g) palm shortening or ghee, softened

⅓ cup (80 ml) maple syrup or honey

1 cup (100 g) almond flour

2 large eggs

¼ cup (60 ml) full-fat coconut milk

2 Anjou, Bartlett, or other pears

Powdered sugar (see page 33), for dusting (optional)

SPECIAL EQUIPMENT

4 (4-inch/10-cm) round tart pans with removable base

YIELD

Four 4-inch (10-cm) tarts

METHOD

1. Preheat the oven to 325°F (163°C).

2. Chill and shape the dough in the tart pans according to the instructions on page 105. Once chilled, place the crusts in the oven and par-bake for 8 minutes. They should be dry to the touch. Remove from the oven (but keep the oven on). Let the crusts cool in the pans while you prepare the rest of the ingredients.

3. Make the frangipane: In a large bowl, whisk together the shortening, maple syrup, flour, and eggs till smooth. Using a spoon, stir in the coconut milk till just incorporated.

4. To assemble: Peel the pears, then cut them in half and core them (leaving the halves intact). Divide the frangipane evenly among the crusts. Gently place a pear half in the center of each tart—no need to push it into the frangipane.

5. Bake for about 25 minutes or till the frangipane is golden and the pears are cooked through. Let cool completely in the pans, then unmold the tarts. Dust with powdered sugar if desired.

6. These tarts are best eaten the day they are made but can be stored, covered, in the fridge for 1 to 2 days. The crusts will soften over time.

Banana   Linzer   Ganache

MINI TARTLET COMBINATIONS

All the crust recipes in this chapter will produce enough dough to make the 12 mini (2-inch/5-cm) crusts needed for each of the filling and crust combinations below. The baking time and temperature are the same for each crust.

INGREDIENTS

1 recipe tart crust dough (type specified in tartlet recipes below)

SPECIAL EQUIPMENT

12-well nonstick mini tart pan

Pastry bag fitted with a ½-inch (12-mm) French or star tip (optional)

YIELD

12 mini tartlets

METHOD

1. Preheat the oven to 325°F (163°C).

2. Press the dough evenly into wells of the mini tart pan to a thickness of about ⅛ inch (3 mm). Trim the excess dough as needed. For all the crusts except the macaroon ones, carefully prick the crusts all over with a fork. Chill in the freezer for 10 minutes.

3. Bake for 15 to 18 minutes or till golden and crisp. Remove from the oven and let cool slightly. Unmold the crusts and set on a wire rack to cool completely. Just before serving, assemble as directed in the recipes that follow.

Lemon Cream Tartlets

INGREDIENTS

1 recipe Lemon Curd (page 52)

12 mini Macaroon Crusts (page 109), prebaked

1 recipe Sweetened Whipped Cream (page 48)

METHOD

Divide the curd evenly among the crusts, then pipe or use a spoon to top each tartlet with a generous amount of whipped cream.

Raspberry Vanilla Crème Tartlets

INGREDIENTS

1 recipe Pastry Cream (page 46)

12 mini Chocolate Macaroon Crusts (page 109), prebaked

1 cup (170 g) fresh raspberries

METHOD

Divide the pastry cream evenly among the crusts, then arrange a few raspberries on top of the cream.

Mocha Ganache Tartlets

INGREDIENTS

1 recipe Mocha Ganache (page 66)

12 mini Macaroon Crusts (page 109), prebaked

12 whole roasted espresso beans, for garnish

METHOD

After making the ganache, allow it to cool to room temperature, following step 5 in the Ganache recipe, then whip it till it is light and fluffy. Generously pipe or scoop the whipped ganache into the crusts, then gently press a roasted coffee bean onto each top.

Banana Cream Tartlets

INGREDIENTS

1 recipe Banana Pastry Cream (page 46)

12 mini Chocolate Crusts (page 107), prebaked

½ recipe Sweetened Whipped Cream (page 48)

12 dried banana chips, for garnish

METHOD

Divide the pastry cream evenly among the crusts, then pipe or use a spoon to top with whipped cream. Garnish each tartlet with a banana chip.

Raspberry Linzer Tartlets

INGREDIENTS

1 recipe Raspberry Jam (page 51) or 1 cup (240 ml) store-bought

12 mini Shortbread Crusts (page 106), prebaked

Powdered sugar (see page 33), for dusting (optional)

METHOD

Divide the jam evenly among the crusts. Dust with powdered sugar just before serving, if desired.

Dark Chocolate Ganache Pecan Tartlets

INGREDIENTS

1 recipe Ganache (page 66)

12 mini Macaroon Crusts (page 109), prebaked

12 whole pecans, toasted, for garnish

METHOD

After making the ganache, let it cool till lukewarm but still pourable. Fill each crust almost to the edge with the ganache. It should smooth out nicely on its own. Gently place a pecan on top of the ganache, but do not press it in. Leave till set.

BUILD YOUR OWN TARTS

PICK A CRUST (pages 106–109)

☐ Shortbread Crust

☐ Chocolate Crust

☐ Nut-Free Sweet Crust

☐ Macaroon Crust

☐ Chocolate Macaroon Crust

PICK A FILLING

Pastry Creams (pages 46–47)

☐ Pastry Cream

☐ Banana Pastry Cream

☐ Matcha Green Tea Pastry Cream

☐ Pistachio Pastry Cream

☐ Praline Pastry Cream

Whipped Creams (pages 48–49)

☐ Sweetened Whipped Cream

☐ Chocolate Whipped Cream

☐ Raspberry Whipped Cream

☐ Espresso Whipped Cream

☐ Matcha Green Tea Whipped Cream

Jams (pages 50–51)

☐ Orange Marmalade

☐ Apricot Jam

☐ Blackberry Jam

☐ Raspberry Jam

Curds (page 52)

☐ Lemon Curd

☐ Passion Fruit Curd

Other Fillings

☐ Zabaglione (page 53)

☐ Whipped Ganache (page 66)

☐ Assortment of berries & fruits

PICK A TOPPING

Whipped Creams (pages 48–49)

☐ Sweetened Whipped Cream

☐ Chocolate Whipped Cream

☐ Raspberry Whipped Cream

☐ Matcha Green Tea Whipped Cream

☐ Espresso Whipped Cream

Other Toppings

☐ Swiss Meringue (page 57)

☐ Assortment of berries & fruits

PICK A GARNISH

☐ Candied bananas (page 84)

☐ Candied bacon (page 93)

☐ Fruits

☐ Nuts

☐ Whatever your creativity inspires

frosting

filling

cake

Chapter 5:

CAKES

For almost every significant moment in our lives, be it a birthday, a wedding, a graduation, or a baby shower, there seems to be a cake. I think this is probably because cakes are inherently celebratory; they make a statement about the significance of that moment. The time it takes to prepare them, their beauty, their flavor, and the overall presentation all reflect the importance of the particular event that has brought a group together. Cakes are the way we say, "This event in your life is important, and we're here to celebrate what has happened, together."

ABOUT CAKES

Many of the cakes in this book are smaller than typical homemade cakes. For instance, the layer cakes are 6-inch (15-cm) cakes unless otherwise noted. This size, which is actually not uncommon for an artisan-style cake, allows us grain-free bakers to focus on making extravagant and beautiful creations, especially since grain-free baking uses calorie-dense ingredients that can be quite expensive.

This chapter starts with basic vanilla and chocolate cake recipes. I've provided both nut flour–based and nut-free versions that can be used interchangeably and are equally delicious. These are the cakes that you would traditionally use for birthdays, weddings, or any other celebratory occasion. I've included a few of my own favorite combinations, but these basic cakes can be combined with any of the fillings, frostings, and glazes from the first two chapters of the book to create mix-and-match desserts ranging from simple to elaborate. The chapter continues on to introduce other types of cakes, which can be used for a variety of different applications.

TIPS FOR MAKING GREAT CAKES

Invest in an oven thermometer. Most ovens do not read their temperature accurately and can be off enough to negatively affect your cakes. Using an oven thermometer will help to ensure the best baking results.

Give the oven at least 20 minutes to preheat to get the most even baking results.

Leave the oven door closed for at least the first three-quarters of the baking time to ensure the best volume and to prevent a sunken or fallen cake.

I recommend purchasing at least two 6-inch (15-cm) round cake pans. They are quite inexpensive and are valuable tools for creating stunning cakes.

Remember, making cakes doesn't necessarily have to be an elaborate production. The basic vanilla and chocolate cake recipes on pages 132–135 can be made as single 6-inch (15-cm) cakes and simply frosted. You can also make a double recipe of batter to fill a single 9-inch (24-cm) cake pan, which can be frosted or cut in half for an easy layer cake. (The 9-inch/24-cm cakes require an additional 5 to 8 minutes of baking time.) These recipes can also made into 8 to 10 cupcakes, using about ¼ cup of batter per cupcake. Bake the cupcakes for 15 to 18 minutes, or a little longer for the coconut flour–based versions, till the top springs back when gently pressed.

Vanilla Cake

The last-minute addition of baking soda and folded-in whipped egg whites gives this cake and its chocolate counterpart (opposite) great volume and a lovely texture. The nut-free version of this cake can be found on page 134.

INGREDIENTS

⅓ cup (65 g) palm shortening or ghee

1¾ cups (175 g) almond flour

¼ cup (30 g) arrowroot flour

¼ teaspoon salt

3 large eggs, room temperature

½ cup (120 ml) maple syrup or honey

2 teaspoons vanilla extract

1 teaspoon lemon juice

½ teaspoon baking soda

YIELD

One single-layer (6-inch/15-cm) round cake

METHOD

1. Preheat the oven to 325°F (163°C). Grease and line a 6-inch round cake pan with a parchment paper circle cut to fit the pan.

2. In a small saucepan, melt the shortening over gentle heat, then set aside to cool slightly. In a large bowl, whisk together the flours and salt till blended.

3. Separate the eggs, placing the whites in a medium-sized bowl or the bowl of a stand mixer. Place the yolks in another bowl along with the melted shortening, maple syrup, vanilla, and lemon juice. Whisk to combine. Add the egg yolk mixture to the large bowl with the flour and whisk till the batter is smooth and no lumps remain.

4. Using a hand mixer or the whisk attachment for your stand mixer, beat the egg whites till they look like softly whipped cream (soft peaks). Stir the baking soda into the batter and then, using a rubber spatula, immediately beat in one-third of the whipped egg whites to lighten the batter. Gently fold in the rest of the egg whites till only a few streaks of egg white are left.

5. If using for layers, pour only 2 cups (475 ml) of the batter into the prepared cake pan, leaving behind about ¼ cup (60 ml). Otherwise, for a single-layer cake to be topped with a glaze, fruit, etc., use all of the batter for a tall, rustic look. Bake for 35 to 40 minutes or till a wooden skewer poked into the center of the cake comes out clean. Leave to set for about 5 minutes, then run a sharp knife around the edge of the cake and turn out onto a cooling rack. Let cool completely.

NOTE

You can bake the excess batter in a small ramekin for a cake sampler. The baking time will be about 20 minutes.

Chocolate Cake

The nut-free version of this cake can be found on page 135.

INGREDIENTS

⅓ cup (65 g) palm shortening or ghee

1¾ cups (175 g) almond flour

⅓ cup (35 g) cocoa powder

¼ teaspoon salt

3 large eggs, room temperature

½ cup (120 ml) maple syrup or honey

2 teaspoons vanilla extract

1 teaspoon apple cider vinegar

½ teaspoon baking soda

YIELD

One single-layer (6-inch/15-cm) round cake

METHOD

1. Preheat the oven to 325°F (163°C). Grease and line a 6-inch round cake pan with a parchment paper circle cut to fit the pan.

2. In a small saucepan, melt the shortening over gentle heat, then set aside to cool slightly. In a large bowl, whisk together the flour, cocoa, and salt till blended.

3. Separate the eggs, placing the whites in a medium-sized bowl or the bowl of a stand mixer. Place the yolks in another bowl along with the melted shortening, maple syrup, vanilla, and vinegar. Whisk to combine. Add the egg yolk mixture to the large bowl with the flour and whisk till the batter is smooth and no lumps remain.

4. Using a hand mixer or the whisk attachment for your stand mixer, beat the egg whites till they look like softly whipped cream (soft peaks). Stir the baking soda into the batter and then, using a rubber spatula, immediately beat in one-third of the whipped egg whites to lighten the batter. Gently fold in the rest of the egg whites till only a few streaks of egg white are left.

5. If using for layers, pour only 2 cups (475 ml) of the batter into the prepared cake pan, leaving behind about ¼ cup (60 ml). Otherwise, for a single-layer cake to be topped with a glaze, fruit, etc., use all of the batter for a tall, rustic look. Bake for 35 to 40 minutes or till a wooden skewer poked into the center of the cake comes out clean. Leave to set for about 5 minutes, then run a sharp knife around the edge of the cake and turn out onto a cooling rack. Let cool completely.

NOTE

You can bake the excess batter in a small ramekin for a cake sampler. The baking time will be about 20 minutes.

Nut-Free Vanilla Cake

This nut-free vanilla cake can be used in any of the recipes that call for vanilla cake.

INGREDIENTS

½ cup (90 g) palm shortening or ghee

½ cup (60 g) coconut flour

¼ teaspoon salt

5 large eggs

½ cup (120 ml) maple syrup or honey

1 teaspoon vanilla extract

2 teaspoons lemon juice

½ teaspoon baking soda

YIELD

One single-layer (6-inch/15-cm) round cake

METHOD

1. Preheat the oven to 325°F (163°C). Grease and line a 6-inch round cake pan with a parchment paper circle cut to fit the pan.

2. In a small saucepan, melt the shortening over gentle heat, then set aside to cool slightly. In a large bowl, whisk together the flour and salt till blended.

3. Separate three of the eggs, placing the whites in a medium-sized bowl or the bowl of a stand mixer. Place the yolks in another bowl along with the two remaining whole eggs, melted shortening, maple syrup, vanilla, and lemon juice. Whisk to combine. Add the egg yolk mixture to the flour mixture and whisk till the batter is smooth and no lumps remain.

4. Using a hand mixer or the whisk attachment for your stand mixer, beat the egg whites till they look like softly whipped cream (soft peaks). Stir the baking soda into the batter and then, using a rubber spatula, immediately beat in one-third of the whipped egg whites to lighten the batter. Gently fold in the rest of the egg whites till only a few streaks of egg white are left.

5. Pour the batter into the prepared pan and bake for 35 to 40 minutes or till a wooden skewer poked into the center of the cake comes out clean. Remove from the oven and let cool in the pan for 10 minutes, then run a sharp knife around the edge of the cake and turn out onto a cooling rack. Let cool completely.

Nut-Free Chocolate Cake

This nut-free chocolate cake can be used in any of the recipes that call for chocolate cake.

INGREDIENTS

¼ cup (45 g) palm shortening or ghee

½ cup (60 g) coconut flour

¼ cup (25 g) cocoa powder

1 tablespoon arrowroot flour

Pinch of salt

3 large eggs, room temperature

½ cup (120 ml) full-fat coconut milk

½ cup (120 ml) maple syrup or honey

1 teaspoon vanilla extract

1 teaspoon apple cider vinegar

¾ teaspoon baking soda

YIELD

One single-layer (6-inch/15-cm) round cake

METHOD

1. Preheat the oven to 325°F (163°C). Grease and line a 6-inch round cake pan with a parchment paper circle cut to fit the pan.

2. In a small saucepan, melt the shortening over gentle heat, then set aside to cool slightly. In a large bowl, whisk together the coconut flour, cocoa, arrowroot flour, and salt till blended.

3. Separate the eggs, placing the whites in a medium-sized bowl or the bowl of a stand mixer. Place the yolks in another bowl along with the milk, maple syrup, vanilla, vinegar, and melted shortening. Whisk to combine. Add the egg yolk mixture to the flour mixture and whisk till the batter is smooth and no lumps remain.

4. Using a hand mixer or the whisk attachment for your stand mixer, beat the egg whites till they look like softly whipped cream (soft peaks). Stir the baking soda into the batter and then, using a rubber spatula, immediately beat in one-third of the whipped egg whites to lighten the batter. Gently fold in the rest of the egg whites till only a few streaks of egg white are left.

5. Pour the batter into the prepared pan and bake for 35 to 40 minutes or till a wooden skewer poked into the center of the cake comes out clean. Remove from the oven and let cool in the pan for 5 minutes, then run a sharp knife around the edge of the cake and turn out onto a cooling rack. Let cool completely.

Chocolate Cherry Naked Cake

Always stunning yet super easy to make, "naked" cakes don't require frosting on the outside. I often fill these cakes with nearly twice the usual amount of filling for an extravagant, eye-catching look, but feel free to use less filling if desired. For this recipe you will need three 6-inch (15-cm) round cake pans, as the recipe is written for that amount of batter. However, this amount of batter will also make one 9-inch (24-cm) round cake for a nice single-layer cake if desired. The cake shown was made with almond flour–based chocolate cake batter (page 133), but you can use the nut-free version on page 135 if you prefer.

INGREDIENTS

Double recipe chocolate cake batter

Triple recipe Chocolate Whipped Cream (page 49)

2 cups (340 g) whole Bing cherries with stems

Cocoa powder, for dusting

YIELD

One three-layer (6-inch/15-cm) round cake (serving 12 to 15)

METHOD

1. Preheat the oven to 325°F (163°C). Grease and line the cake pans with parchment paper circles cut to fit the pans.

2. Divide the cake batter evenly among the pans, using about 1½ cups (375 ml) of batter per pan. Bake for about 25 minutes or till a wooden skewer poked in the center of the cake comes out clean. Remove from the oven and let rest for 5 minutes. Run a sharp knife around the edge of each pan, then turn the cakes out onto a cooling rack. Let cool completely. These cakes should not need any trimming.

3. When ready to assemble, slice about ½ cup (85 g) of the cherries in half and pull out the pits. Place the first cake layer on the plate or base on which you will be serving it. Pile a generous amount of the whipped cream filling (about ¾ cup/185 ml) onto the cake. Sprinkle some halved cherries on top of the whipped cream, then gently place the second cake layer on top. Pile another cup of filling on top and add the rest of the halved cherries. Finally, place the last cake layer and pile more filling on the top of the cake in a decorative manner. Garnish the cake with handfuls of whole cherries, piling them as high as you can get away with. Using a sifter or small fine-mesh sieve, dust some cocoa on top.

NOTE

Be creative and use this recipe as a model for other cakes. Simply follow the same instructions, replacing the cakes, fillings or frostings, and garnishes with any combination of flavors you like.

Neapolitan Cake

A delicious combination of chocolate and vanilla cakes layered with raspberry buttercream. The cake shown was made with the nut-free vanilla and chocolate cakes on pages 134 and 135, but you can use the almond flour–based cakes on pages 132 and 133 if you prefer.

INGREDIENTS

1 (6-inch/15-cm) chocolate cake

1 (6-inch/15-cm) vanilla cake

Double recipe Raspberry Meringue Buttercream (page 59)

SPECIAL EQUIPMENT

Large pastry bag fitted with a ½-inch (1.25-cm) round tip

YIELD

One four-layer (6-inch/15-cm) round cake (serving 10 to 12)

NOTE

For nicer-looking layers that require little or no trimming, you can bake the batter in two 6-inch (15-cm) pans for about 20 minutes or till the cakes spring back when gently pressed.

METHOD

1. Check the cakes to make sure they are level. If not, use a large serrated knife to shave the tops slightly, making them level. Slice the cakes in half to make four thin layers, unless you made the thinner layers as described in the Note below.

2. Place one of the chocolate cake layers in the center of a serving dish or cake stand. Spread a thick layer of buttercream (about ⅓ cup/80 ml) evenly over the cake and out toward the edges. Lay a vanilla cake layer on top and press down slightly to secure it. Spread another thick layer of frosting on top of that layer, then top it with a chocolate cake layer. Repeat these steps, finishing with the second vanilla cake layer. Make sure to place this final layer trimmed side down so the top of the cake is smooth.

3. Frost the outside of the cake with an even coat of buttercream, reserving most of the frosting for decorating. It's okay if a little cake shows through here and there; it will be covered later. Pay special attention to the top of the cake, though, using extra frosting and smoothing it out or giving it the texture you want the finished version to have.

4. To decorate (see pages 276–277 for photo instructions), fill the pastry bag with the remaining frosting and pipe a row of five or six vertical dots down the side of the cake. Place the tip of an offset spatula or butter knife against the middle of the first dot. Tilt the handle slightly toward the cake and pull some of the icing with the spatula to create a "petal" with a thin edge. Repeat this process with the rest of the dots, then start another row of dots at the end of the row you just pulled. Continue making rows of dots till the whole cake is covered. For the top of the cake, pipe a layer of dots around the circumference, pulling them toward the center of the cake. Use a damp towel to clean any frosting off the serving plate.

5. This cake is great at room temperature or chilled. It can be stored, covered, in the fridge for up to 2 days.

Sacher Torte

Sacher torte is a classic Austrian chocolate cake layered with apricot preserves. It is traditionally served with a side of whipped cream, but is equally delicious on its own. The torte shown was made with nut-free chocolate cake (page 135), but you can use the almond flour–based version on page 133 if you prefer.

INGREDIENTS

1 (6-inch/15-cm) chocolate cake

1 cup (240 ml) Apricot Jam (page 51) or store-bought

1 recipe Sweet Chocolate Glaze (page 67)

1 recipe Sweetened Whipped Cream (page 48), for serving

YIELD

One filled (6-inch/15-cm) round cake (serving 6)

METHOD

1. When ready to assemble the torte, slice the cake in half. Place the bottom layer on a wire rack. Soften ½ cup (120 ml) of the jam in a small bowl by stirring and pressing with a spoon. Spread the jam over the cake layer. You may not need all of it. Place the other cake layer on top, pressing down slightly to secure it.

2. In a small saucepan over medium-high heat, bring the remaining ½ cup (120 ml) of jam to a simmer, stirring every once in a while. Once it becomes liquid, press it through a fine-mesh sieve.

3. Place the rack with the cake on it over a rimmed baking sheet to catch drips. Starting at the center of the cake, pour on the apricot glaze, letting it move outward. Again, you may not need all of it. Use a spatula or spoon to spread the glaze in a thin layer over the entire surface of the cake. You don't want the glaze to be too thick. Leave till the glaze is set, about 15 minutes.

4. Prepare the chocolate glaze. With the cake still set over the baking sheet, start at the center of the cake and pour on the chocolate glaze. Pick up and tilt the cake as needed to help the chocolate cover the entire surface of the cake. Add more chocolate on the edges as needed. Chill the cake in the fridge for about 20 minutes to quick-set the glaze. This will make it easier to transfer it to a plate for serving.

5. Transfer the cake to a 7-inch (18-cm) or larger plate or cake stand. Serve each slice with a dollop of whipped cream.

Chocolate Bundt Cake with Blackberries

The cake shown was made with almond flour–based chocolate cake batter (page 133), but you can use the nut-free version on page 135 if you prefer.

INGREDIENTS

Double recipe chocolate cake batter

½ recipe Ganache (page 66)

1 cup (170 g) fresh blackberries, for garnish

SPECIAL EQUIPMENT

1 (3 by 8.5-inch / 7.5 by 22-cm) nonstick Bundt pan or other 6-cup (1.4-L) capacity Bundt pan

SERVES

8 to 10

METHOD

1. Preheat the oven to 325°F (163°C) and grease the Bundt pan.

2. Prepare the cake batter and immediately pour it into the prepared pan. Bake for about 40 minutes, till the top is golden and springs back when gently pressed at the center. Baking times can vary slightly depending on the pan. Check the cake in the last 10 minutes of baking to see how it has progressed. Remove from the oven and let cool for 10 minutes. Loosen the edges with a sharp knife, then unmold onto a wire rack and let cool completely.

3. While the cake cools, prepare the ganache and allow it to cool to room temperature. (It will glaze best at room temperature, so give it some time to cool down, but not so much time that it is no longer pourable.)

4. Place the rack with the cake on it over a baking sheet or piece of parchment paper to catch drips. Drizzle the ganache over the cake in a decorative manner. Once the glaze has set, pile the blackberries on top of the cake, allowing them to fill up the center hole.

5. The cake can be kept, covered, in the fridge for up to 2 days.

Vanilla Lavender Bundt Cake with Vanilla Glaze

The cake shown was made with almond flour–based cake batter (page 132), but you can use the nut-free version on page 134 if you prefer.

INGREDIENTS

Double recipe vanilla cake batter

2 teaspoons dried lavender flowers, plus more for garnish

1 recipe Vanilla Coconut Butter Glaze (page 64)

SPECIAL EQUIPMENT

1 (3 by 8.5-inch / 7.5 by 22-cm) nonstick Bundt pan or other 6-cup (1.4-L) capacity Bundt pan

SERVES

8 to 10

METHOD

1. Preheat the oven to 325°F (163°C) and grease the Bundt pan.

2. Prepare the cake batter, then fold in the lavender flowers. Immediately pour the batter into the prepared pan and bake for about 40 minutes, till the top is golden and springs back when gently pressed at the center. Baking times can vary slightly depending on the pan. Check the cake in the last 10 minutes of baking to see how it has progressed. Remove from the oven and let cool in the pan for about 10 minutes. Loosen the edges with a sharp knife, then unmold onto a wire rack and let cool completely.

3. Place the rack with the cake on it over a baking sheet or piece of parchment paper to catch drips. Prepare the glaze and either drizzle or pour it over the cake in a decorative manner. Place the cake in the freezer for a maximum of 5 minutes to set the glaze. If it doesn't fit in your freezer, chill the cake in the fridge for about 30 minutes or till the glaze has set. At that point you can either leave it in the fridge or let it sit out at room temperature before serving. Both ways are delicious.

4. The cake can be kept, covered, in the fridge for up to 2 days.

Joconde Cake

Joconde cake is a traditional almond flour–based sponge-style cake baked in thin rectangular layers. Though it has many uses, in this book it is used mainly for opera cake (page 151) and cake rolls (page 153).

INGREDIENTS

2 tablespoons palm shortening or ghee

1 cup plus 2 tablespoons (115 g) almond flour

¼ cup (30 g) arrowroot flour

½ cup plus 1 tablespoon (115 g) firmly packed maple sugar

3 large egg whites, room temperature

3 large eggs

⅛ teaspoon cream of tartar

SPECIAL EQUIPMENT

15 by 10-inch (38 by 25-cm) jelly roll pan

YIELD

One 15 by 10-inch (38 by 25-cm) cake

METHOD

1. Preheat the oven to 425°F (218°C). Grease and line the jelly roll pan with parchment paper, then grease the top of the parchment paper as well.

2. In a small saucepan, melt the shortening over medium heat, then set aside to cool. Pulse the sugar in a small coffee/spice grinder until fine and powdery and set aside 3 tablespoons. A very fine sugar is important to the texture of the cake.

3. Sift the flours and sugar together into a bowl and set aside.

4. In the bowl of a stand mixer fitted with a whisk attachment, whip the egg whites till foamy, then add the cream of tartar and continue beating until the mixture looks like softly whipped cream (soft peaks). Add the 3 tablespoons of reserved sugar, then beat on medium-high speed till stiff peaks form. Scrape the meringue into a separate clean bowl.

5. Return the bowl to the mixer stand (no need to clean it out) and switch to the paddle attachment. Place the flour mixture and the three whole eggs in the bowl and beat on medium-high speed till light and increased in volume, about 3 minutes. Remove the bowl from the mixer stand and gently fold in the egg whites till only a few white streaks remain. Then gently fold in the cooled shortening.

6. Transfer the batter to the prepared pan, spreading it evenly. Bake for 6 to 8 minutes or till the cake has golden flecks and the top springs back when gently pressed.

7. If using for opera cake (and other layer cakes): Remove the cake from the oven and let cool in the pan for a few minutes, then loosen the edges with a sharp knife and turn out onto a cooling rack. Let cool completely before using.

8. If using for cake rolls: Lay out a large flour sack towel on your work surface. Using a small sifter, dust the surface of the towel lightly with arrowroot flour (or cocoa for the chocolate variation below). As soon as you remove the cake from the oven, loosen the edges with a sharp knife, then turn it out onto the towel. Remove the parchment paper. With the short end facing you, tightly roll up the cake in the towel, rolling away from you. Rolling tightly helps support the cake as it cools and helps to prevent cracking. Let cool completely before using.

Flavor Variations for Joconde Cake:

Hazelnut Joconde Cake.
Replace the almond flour with an equal amount of hazelnut flour.

Chocolate Joconde Cake.
Use four egg whites instead of three and replace ¼ cup (30 g) of the almond flour with cocoa powder. Instead of powdered sugar, dust the surface of the towel with cocoa.

Opera Cake

This classic cake is made with layers of coffee-soaked hazelnut sponge cake, coffee buttercream, and ganache. See pages 278–279 for photo instructions.

INGREDIENTS

For the coffee syrup:

¾ cup (185 ml) water

½ cup (120 ml) maple syrup or honey

2 tablespoons instant espresso coffee or espresso powder

2 Hazelnut Joconde Cakes (pages 148–149)

1 recipe Coffee French Buttercream (page 60)

1 recipe Extra-Thick Ganache (page 66)

For the chocolate glaze:

5 ounces (140 g) bittersweet chocolate (70% cacao or higher), finely chopped

1½ tablespoons palm shortening or ghee

SERVES

10

METHOD

1. Make the coffee syrup: Whisk together the water, maple syrup, and espresso in a small saucepan. Bring just to a boil over high heat, then remove from the heat and let cool completely.

2. Prepare the remaining elements for the opera cake. Keep all the elements covered and at room temperature till ready to assemble.

3. To assemble: Trim the joconde cakes so that the edges are nice and even, then cut them in half, making four rectangles altogether. The dimensions are less important than equal sizing. Place the first cake layer in the center of a cookie sheet. Using a pastry brush, soak the cake in coffee syrup. Then spread about ¼ inch (6 mm) of buttercream evenly over the surface of the cake.

4. Apply the next cake layer, soak it in coffee syrup, and then spread the ganache over the cake in a thin layer.

5. Apply the next layer of cake and soak it in syrup, then add another layer of buttercream. Don't worry if it's a bit sloppy at the edges; they will be trimmed later.

6. Place the last cake layer on top and soak it in syrup. Apply a very thin layer of buttercream—just enough to fill in any pits in the cake to make a smooth base for the final chocolate glaze. Make it as smooth as possible.

7. Make the chocolate glaze: Heat the chocolate and shortening in a bowl over simmering water, stirring till just melted. Pour it into the center of the cake and use a spatula to spread it outward to cover the top of the cake.

8. Chill the fully assembled cake for at least 1 hour, then use a knife dipped in hot water and dried to trim the edges. Then cut the cake into 10 even slices.

9. Opera cake is best served slightly chilled. Leftover cake can be stored, covered, in the fridge for up to 2 days.

CAKE ROLLS

For photo instructions, see pages 280–281.

Raspberry-Glazed Vanilla Cake Roll

INGREDIENTS

1 Joconde Cake (pages 148–149)

1 recipe Sweetened Whipped Cream (page 48)

1 recipe Raspberry Fondant Glaze (page 63)

SERVES

6 to 8

METHOD

1. After removing the cake from the oven, form it into a roll, following step 8 in the Joconde Cake recipe.

2. When ready to assemble the cake roll, carefully unroll the cooled cake toward you while supporting the bottom to help prevent it from cracking. Spread the whipped cream over the top, leaving a ½-inch (1.25-cm) margin around the edges. Reroll the cake, using a towel to help guide the cake into a nice even roll. Refrigerate for about 30 minutes before glazing.

3. Make the glaze, then remove the cake from the fridge and place it on a wire rack. Set the rack over a baking sheet or piece of parchment paper to catch drips, then drizzle or pour the glaze evenly over the cake. Place the cake back in the fridge and chill till set.

4. This cake is best served within a few hours of assembly but can be stored, covered, in the fridge for up to 2 days.

Chocolate & Espresso Cake Roll

INGREDIENTS

1 Chocolate Joconde Cake (pages 148–149)

1 recipe Espresso Whipped Cream (page 49)

½ recipe Ganache (page 66)

SERVES

6 to 8

METHOD

1. After removing the cake from the oven, form it into a roll, following step 8 in the Joconde Cake recipe.

2. When ready to assemble the cake roll, carefully unroll the cooled cake toward you while supporting the bottom to help prevent it from cracking. Spread the whipped cream over the top, leaving a ½-inch (1.25-cm) margin around the edges. Reroll the cake, using a towel to help guide the cake into a nice even roll. Refrigerate for about 30 minutes before glazing.

3. Make the ganache, then remove the cake from the fridge and place it on a wire rack. Set the rack over a baking sheet or piece of parchment paper to catch drips, then drizzle or pour the ganache evenly over the cake. Place the cake back in the fridge and chill till set.

4. This cake is best served within a few hours of assembly but can be stored, covered, in the fridge for up to 2 days.

Maple Carrot Cake

For this recipe you will need three 6-inch (15-cm) round cake pans, as the recipe is written for that amount of batter. However, this amount of batter will also make one 9-inch (24-cm) round cake for a nice single-layer cake if desired.

INGREDIENTS

For the cake:

¼ cup (45 g) palm shortening or ghee

4 large eggs

1 large egg white

1 cup (200 g) firmly packed maple sugar

1 teaspoon lemon juice

3½ cups (350 g) almond flour

1 teaspoon ground cinnamon

¾ teaspoon ginger powder

½ teaspoon ground nutmeg

½ teaspoon baking soda

½ cup (40 g) unsweetened shredded coconut

⅓ cup (50 g) raisins

⅓ cup (60 g) chopped pineapple

⅓ cup (40 g) chopped pecans

3 medium carrots (260 g), grated

1 recipe Swiss Meringue Buttercream (page 58)

3 cups (170 g) coconut flakes, for garnish

YIELD

One three-layer (6-inch/15-cm) round cake (serving 12 to 15)

METHOD

1. Preheat the oven to 325°F (163°C). Grease and line the cake pans with parchment paper circles cut to fit the pans.

2. Melt the shortening in a small saucepan over low heat, then set aside to cool. In the bowl of a stand mixer fitted with a whisk attachment, beat the eggs, egg white, sugar, and lemon juice on medium-high speed for 15 minutes. The mixture should become thick and voluminous. Always beat it for the whole 15 minutes, though.

3. While the egg mixture is beating, whisk together the flour, spices, and baking soda in a large bowl till blended. Add the shredded coconut, raisins, pineapple, pecans, carrots, and melted shortening, then toss to combine.

4. When the egg mixture is ready, gently fold it into the flour mixture till completely incorporated. Divide the batter evenly among the prepared pans and bake for 30 to 35 minutes or till the tops spring back when gently pressed. (Bake for 35 to 40 minutes if using a 9-inch/24-cm round cake pan.)

5. Remove from the oven and let cool in the pans for about 10 minutes. Loosen the edge of each cake with a sharp knife, then turn the cakes out onto a wire rack and let cool completely before frosting.

6. To assemble: Place the first cake layer on a plate or cake stand. Spread about a ¼-inch (6-mm)-thick layer of buttercream evenly over the cake. Place the second cake layer on top of the buttercream, then spread more buttercream on top. Finally, place the last cake layer, then frost the top and sides of the cake with the remaining buttercream. You don't need a super thick layer, but you want enough buttercream to press the coconut flakes into.

7. Scoop up handfuls of coconut flakes and gently press them into and all over the surface of the cake.

8. For best results, chill the cake, uncovered, for about 30 minutes to secure the coconut flakes. If needed, fill in gaps by placing a little frosting on the back of a coconut flake and secure it to the area.

Tiramisù

Tiramisù is an Italian dessert that is flavored primarily with coffee and often brandy. Due to its incredibly versatile nature, tiramisù can be made in anything from a bowl to a pan to little cups. It's all about the layers. So get creative.

INGREDIENTS

1 cup (240 ml) espresso

1 tablespoon maple syrup or honey

1 tablespoon brandy (optional)

1 recipe Zabaglione (page 53)

1 recipe Ladyfingers (page 185)

½ cup (50 g) cocoa powder

SERVES

6 to 8

METHOD

1. Have on hand a 9 by 5-inch (23 by 12.75-cm) loaf pan for a four-layer tiramisù as shown.

2. Place the espresso in a small bowl. Add the maple syrup and brandy, if using, and stir to combine. Make the zabaglione, then dip the bottom of each ladyfinger in the coffee for just a few seconds. Arrange the coffee-dipped ladyfingers to cover the bottom of the loaf pan.

3. Spread a layer of zabaglione over the soaked ladyfingers—about ¾ cup (185 ml), but it's not a science. Using a small sifter or fine-mesh sieve, dust with a thick layer of cocoa, then arrange another layer of coffee-dipped ladyfingers. Add more zabaglione on top of the ladyfingers and dust with more cocoa. Repeat this process two more times or till all the ladyfingers are used up. Dust the top with a final layer of cocoa.

4. Cover and chill for at least 2 hours, then scoop or cut into serving dishes. Tiramisù will keep in the fridge, covered, for about 2 days.

Madeleines

These are classic sponge-style cakes baked in small shell-shaped molds.

INGREDIENTS

¼ cup (60 g) ghee or palm shortening

1 cup (100 g) almond flour

3 tablespoons arrowroot flour

¼ teaspoon baking soda

¼ teaspoon salt

2 large eggs, room temperature

⅓ cup (40 g) firmly packed maple sugar

Grated zest of 1 lemon

SPECIAL EQUIPMENT

Stainless-steel 12-cavity madeleine pan with 3½-inch (9-cm) molds

YIELD

12 madeleines

METHOD

1. Melt the ghee in a small saucepan, then set aside to cool. Sift the flours, baking soda, and salt into a bowl.

2. Using a stand mixer fitted with a whisk attachment, beat the eggs and sugar on high speed for 5 minutes, till pale, thick, and voluminous. Add the lemon zest, then whisk for another 2 minutes. Using a rubber spatula, gently fold the flour mixture into the whipped egg mixture in two additions. Once combined, fold in the melted ghee in two additions. Do not overmix the batter, or it will deflate and lose its volume. Cover and chill for at least 2 hours or overnight.

3. Preheat the oven to 375°F (190°C). Generously grease the madeleine pan. Chill the pan in the freezer while the oven preheats.

4. Add about 1 rounded tablespoon of chilled batter to each mold. Bake for about 10 minutes or till the tops spring back when gently pressed and the edges are golden and crispy. Let cool for a few minutes, then use the tip of a small knife to remove the madeleines from the molds and transfer to a cooling rack.

5. Madeleines become dense when stored, so they are best enjoyed while still warm or later the same day. The batter can be stored in the fridge for several days, so you can bake them in smaller batches at your leisure.

VARIATION: PISTACHIO/HAZELNUT MADELEINES

Substitute an equal amount of pistachio or hazelnut flour for the almond flour and omit the lemon zest.

There is nothing more delightful than madeleines fresh out of the oven. However, they are also delicious with glazes. Here are a few of my favorite pairings.

As pictured from top to bottom:

Hazelnut Madeleine with Raspberry Fondant Glaze (page 63)

Classic Madeleine with Maple Fondant Glaze (page 62)

Pistachio Madeleine with Ganache (page 66)

To glaze the madeleines, let the cakes cool completely, then dip or drizzle each one in the glaze, allowing the excess to drip back into the bowl. Place on a wire rack or sheet of parchment paper till set.

BUILD YOUR OWN CAKES

PICK A CAKE

Basic Cakes (pages 132–135)

☐ Vanilla Cake

☐ Chocolate Cake

☐ Nut-Free Vanilla Cake

☐ Nut-Free Chocolate Cake

Joconde Cakes (pages 148–149)

☐ Joconde Cake

☐ Chocolate Joconde Cake

☐ Hazelnut Joconde Cake

PICK A FILLING

Pastry Creams (pages 46–47)

☐ Pastry Cream

☐ Banana Pastry Cream

☐ Matcha Green Tea Pastry Cream

☐ Pistachio Pastry Cream

☐ Praline Pastry Cream

Whipped Creams (pages 48–49)

☐ Sweetened Whipped Cream

☐ Chocolate Whipped Cream

☐ Raspberry Whipped Cream

☐ Matcha Green Tea Whipped Cream

☐ Espresso Whipped Cream

Jams (pages 50–51)

☐ Orange Marmalade

☐ Apricot Jam

☐ Blackberry Jam

☐ Raspberry Jam

Curds (page 52)

☐ Lemon Curd

☐ Passion Fruit Curd

Other Fillings

☐ Zabaglione (page 53)

☐ Whipped Ganache (page 66)

PICK A FROSTING OR GLAZE

Buttercreams (pages 58–61)

☐ Swiss Meringue Buttercream

☐ Raspberry Meringue Buttercream

☐ Chocolate Meringue Buttercream

☐ Espresso Meringue Buttercream

☐ French Buttercream

☐ Coffee French Buttercream

☐ Egg-Free Whipped Buttercream

☐ Raspberry Whipped Buttercream

☐ Coffee Whipped Buttercream

Glazes (pages 62–67)

☐ Maple Fondant Glaze

☐ Chocolate Fondant Glaze

☐ Raspberry Fondant Glaze

☐ Espresso Fondant Glaze

☐ Matcha Green Tea Fondant Glaze

☐ Lemon Fondant Glaze

☐ Key Lime Fondant Glaze

☐ Vanilla Coconut Butter Glaze

☐ Chocolate Coconut Butter Glaze

☐ Espresso Coconut Butter Glaze

☐ Tart Raspberry Coconut Butter Glaze

☐ Lemon Coconut Butter Glaze

☐ Ganache

☐ Sweet Chocolate Glaze

Chapter 6:

COOKIES

Very few things in life are more universal than the love of cookies. There is an inherent spontaneity in making them: pulling out the ingredients, mixing up the dough, smelling them as they bake, and then finally pulling them out of the oven and burning your fingers because you are so eager to taste them. Cookies are the perfect shared moment; they are the memories we hold dear; they are the simple things of life. To me, cookies just represent home.

Cinnamon Raisin Cookies

INGREDIENTS

1¼ cups (130 g) almond flour

2 tablespoons arrowroot flour

½ cup (40 g) unsweetened shredded coconut

1 teaspoon ground cinnamon

½ teaspoon ground nutmeg

¼ teaspoon salt

¼ teaspoon baking soda

½ cup (90 g) palm shortening or ghee, softened

½ cup (100 g) firmly packed maple sugar

1 large egg

2 teaspoons vanilla extract

1 tablespoon full-fat coconut milk

¼ cup (40 g) raisins

SPECIAL EQUIPMENT

Small mechanical ice cream scoop or 2-tablespoon measuring scoop

YIELD

10 large cookies

METHOD

1. Preheat the oven to 350°F (177°C). Grease and line two large cookie sheets with parchment paper. Greasing is important here, as it keeps the parchment from curling. This ensures that the cookies will spread out smoothly.

2. In a small bowl, whisk together the flours, shredded coconut, spices, salt, and baking soda till blended.

3. In the bowl of a stand mixer fitted with a paddle attachment, or with a hand mixer, cream the shortening and sugar on high speed for about 2 minutes, scraping down the sides of the bowl as needed. Add the egg and vanilla and beat to combine. Turn the mixer down to low speed, then add the flour mixture and milk and mix till fully combined. Stir in the raisins.

4. Using the scoop, place slightly rounded mounds of dough on the lined cookie sheets, spacing them at least 4 inches (10 cm) apart. You can fit about 5 per cookies per sheet, leaving room for them to spread as they bake.

5. Bake for 10 to 12 minutes or till golden and crispy on the edges. Remove from the oven and let cool on the pan for 5 minutes, then carefully transfer to a cooling rack.

6. These cookies are best eaten the day they are made and will lose their crispness over the course of the day. But if needed, they can be stored in an airtight container in the fridge for a few days.

Cocoa Ginger Cookies

INGREDIENTS

2 cups (200 g) almond flour

¼ teaspoon salt

¼ rounded teaspoon baking soda

2 teaspoons ground cinnamon

1½ teaspoons ginger powder

1 teaspoon ground nutmeg

1 tablespoon cocoa powder

¼ cup (45 g) palm shortening or ghee, softened

2 tablespoons molasses

3 tablespoons maple syrup or honey

1 tablespoon vanilla extract

½ cup (100 g) coarse sugar, for rolling

SPECIAL EQUIPMENT

Small mechanical ice cream scoop or 2-tablespoon measuring scoop

YIELD

10 cookies

METHOD

1. Preheat the oven to 350°F (177°C). Line a cookie sheet with parchment paper.

2. In a large bowl, whisk together the flour, salt, baking soda, spices, and cocoa till blended. Add the remaining ingredients and stir with a rubber spatula or wooden spoon till fully combined. Pour the coarse sugar into a shallow bowl for rolling.

3. Scoop out level amounts of dough, roll into smooth balls, and then coat each ball in the coarse sugar. Place the balls of dough at least 2 inches (5 cm) apart on the lined cookie sheet. Using your fingers, press down gently on the top of each cookie, flattening it into about a 2-inch (5-cm) round.

4. Bake for about 9 minutes, till crisp around the edges. Remove from the oven and let cool on the pan for a few minutes, then transfer to a cooling rack.

5. These cookies are best eaten the day they are made but can be stored in an airtight container in the fridge for a few days.

VARIATION: TRADITIONAL GINGER SNAPS

Prepare the recipe as directed, but omit the cocoa powder.

Snickerdoodle-Style Cookies

INGREDIENTS

2 cups (200 g) almond flour

2 tablespoons arrowroot flour

¼ teaspoon salt

¼ teaspoon baking soda

¼ cup (45 g) palm shortening or ghee, softened

3 tablespoons maple syrup or honey

1 tablespoon vanilla extract

1 teaspoon lemon juice

⅓ cup (40 g) ground cinnamon, for rolling

SPECIAL EQUIPMENT

Small mechanical ice cream scoop or 2-tablespoon measuring scoop

YIELD

10 cookies

METHOD

1. Preheat the oven to 350°F (177°C). Line a cookie sheet with parchment paper.

2. In a large bowl, whisk together the flours, salt, and baking soda till blended. Add the remaining ingredients and stir with a rubber spatula or wooden spoon till fully combined. Pour the cinnamon into a shallow bowl for rolling.

3. Scoop out level amounts of dough, roll into smooth balls, and then coat each ball in the cinnamon. Place the balls of dough at least 2 inches (5 cm) apart on the lined cookie sheet. Using your fingers, press down gently on the top of each cookie, flattening it into about a 2-inch (5-cm) round.

4. Bake for about 9 minutes, till golden around the edges. Remove from the oven and let cool on the pan for a few minutes, then transfer to a cooling rack.

5. These cookies are best eaten the day they are made but can be stored in an airtight container in the fridge for a few days.

Italian Almond Cookies

This classic cookie is soft on the inside and crisp on the outside. It is often coated with almonds, and here I even have a pistachio variation.

INGREDIENTS

2 cups (200 g) almond flour

⅔ cup (140 g) firmly packed maple sugar

2 large egg whites

Pinch of salt

A few drops of almond extract

For the coating:

1 large egg white

½ cup (45 g) sliced almonds

YIELD

12 cookies

METHOD

1. Preheat the oven to 325°F (163°C). Line a cookie sheet with parchment paper.

2. Combine the flour and sugar in a large bowl. In a separate bowl, beat the two egg whites with a pinch of salt and a few drops of almond extract till they form soft peaks. Using a spatula, fold the beaten egg whites into the flour mixture, mixing till a smooth ball of dough has formed.

3. Make the coating: In a small bowl, beat the egg white with a fork for about 15 seconds. Place the sliced almonds on a small plate or in a shallow bowl. Set aside.

4. Divide the dough into 12 equal portions and shape them into small ovals, about 1½ inches (4 cm) long. You may need to wet and clean your hands periodically, as the dough will be slightly sticky.

5. Coat one cookie at a time on all sides with the beaten egg white, then roll or press in the sliced almonds. Arrange the cookies on the prepared cookie sheet, spacing them about 1 inch (2.5 cm) apart.

6. Bake for 25 to 30 minutes or till golden. Rotate the pan halfway through the baking time for even baking. Let cool on the pan.

7. These cookies are best eaten the day they are made but can be stored in an airtight container at room temperature for up to 3 days.

VARIATION: ITALIAN PISTACHIO COOKIES

This version uses a combination of almond and pistachio flours and chopped pistachios instead of sliced almonds for the coating. Follow the instructions above, but reduce the amount of almond flour to 1 cup (100 g) and add 1 cup (100 g) of pistachio flour. Replace the sliced almonds with ½ cup (65 g) of roughly chopped raw pistachio meats.

Extra-Thin Chocolate Chunk Cookies

INGREDIENTS

1 cup (100 g) almond flour

2 tablespoons arrowroot flour

¼ teaspoon salt

¼ teaspoon baking soda

½ cup (90 g) palm shortening or ghee, softened

½ cup (100 g) firmly packed maple sugar

1 large egg

1 tablespoon vanilla extract

1 tablespoon full-fat coconut milk

½ cup (3 ounces/85 g) chocolate chunks

SPECIAL EQUIPMENT

Small mechanical ice cream scoop or 2-tablespoon measuring scoop

YIELD

10 large cookies

METHOD

1. Preheat the oven to 350°F (177°C). Grease and line two large cookie sheets with parchment paper. Greasing is important here, as it keeps the parchment from curling and ensures that the cookies will spread out smoothly.

2. Sift the almond flour into a small bowl (lumps will cause the cookies to spread unevenly), then add the arrowroot flour, salt, and baking soda and whisk to combine.

3. In the bowl of a stand mixer fitted with a paddle attachment, or with a hand mixer, cream the shortening and sugar on high speed for at least 2 minutes. Scrape down the sides of the bowl as needed. Add the egg and vanilla and beat to combine. Turn the mixer down to low speed, then add the flour mixture and milk and mix till fully combined.

4. Using the scoop, place slightly rounded mounds of dough on the lined cookie sheets, spacing them at least 4 inches (10 cm) apart. You can fit about 5 cookies per sheet, giving them plenty of room to spread as they bake.

5. Bake one sheet at a time for 4 minutes, then open the oven door and, leaving the pan in the oven, sprinkle chocolate chunks evenly over the surface of each cookie. They should fall and deflate some. Try to avoid putting chocolate chunks on the edges, or the cookies will slide into odd shapes as they melt.

6. Close the oven door and continue baking for another 6 to 8 minutes or till golden and crispy around the edges. Remove from the oven and let cool on the pan for about 5 minutes, then carefully transfer to a cooling rack. If the cookies are too soft for your liking once cooled, just pop them back in the oven for a few more minutes.

7. These cookies are best eaten the day they are made and will lose their crispness over the course of the day. But if needed, they can be stored in an airtight container in the fridge for a few days.

Chocolate Swirl Meringues

INGREDIENTS

3 large egg whites (90 g), room temperature

¾ cup (150 g) firmly packed maple sugar

1 teaspoon vanilla extract

¼ teaspoon apple cider vinegar

8 ounces (225 g) bittersweet chocolate, melted and cooled

YIELD

6 large meringues

METHOD

1. Preheat the oven to 250°F (121°C). Line a cookie sheet with parchment paper.

2. Place the egg whites in the bowl of a stand mixer fitted with a whisk attachment. Beat on medium speed till soft peaks form. Sprinkle in the sugar, then add the vanilla and vinegar. Increase the mixer speed to high and beat till the sugar has completely dissolved and the meringue holds stiff glossy peaks.

3. Drizzle some of the cooled chocolate over the meringue, but do not stir it in. The swirl will be mostly on the outside, though some will sink into the cookies. Scoop out 6 large spoonfuls of the meringue, drizzling on more chocolate before scooping each one, and drop them onto the lined cookie sheet, spacing them about 2 inches (5 cm) apart.

4. Bake the meringues for 40 to 50 minutes or till they easily peel off of the parchment paper. Turn off the oven, crack open the oven door, and let the meringues cool in the oven for about 1 hour.

5. These cookies are best eaten the day they are made but can be stored in an airtight container in the fridge for a few days.

Linzer Cookies

INGREDIENTS

1½ cups (160 g) almond flour

1 cup (100 g) hazelnut flour

3 tablespoons arrowroot flour

¼ teaspoon salt

⅓ cup (65 g) palm shortening or ghee, softened

⅓ cup (70 g) firmly packed maple sugar

½ teaspoon vanilla extract

1 large egg

Grated zest of 1 lemon

½ recipe Raspberry Jam (page 51) or ½ cup (120 ml) store-bought

¼ cup (30 g) powdered sugar (see page 33), for dusting (optional)

SPECIAL EQUIPMENT

3-inch (7.5-cm) round or scalloped cookie cutter

1-inch (2.5-cm) round cookie cutter (I just use the back of a large pastry tip)

YIELD

About 8 sandwich cookies

METHOD

1. In a large bowl, whisk together the flours and salt. In a medium-sized bowl, using a hand mixer, cream the shortening and sugar for about 2 minutes. Beat in the vanilla, egg, and zest till well combined. Transfer the shortening mixture to the bowl with the flour mixture and, using a rubber spatula, stir by hand till a dough has come together. Gather the dough into a smooth ball and cover with plastic wrap. Chill for 20 minutes or till firm enough to roll out.

2. Preheat the oven to 350°F (177°C).

3. Lay a large piece of parchment paper on your work surface and lightly dust it with arrowroot flour. Remove the dough from the refrigerator and place it on the floured parchment. Lightly dust the top of the dough with arrowroot flour. Using a rolling pin, roll out the dough to a thickness of about ⅛ inch (3 mm). Dust the dough with more flour if it sticks to the rolling pin.

4. Using the larger round or scalloped cookie cutter, cut out 8 circles, then carefully remove the dough around the cutouts. Gather the excess dough into a ball, wrap in plastic, and set aside.

5. Slide the piece of parchment paper with the cutouts on it onto a cookie sheet. Place the cookie sheet in the freezer for about 5 minutes to help the cutouts retain their shape. Once chilled, remove from the freezer, peel each cutout from the parchment, and place on a new parchment-lined cookie sheet, spaced about 1 inch (2.5 cm) apart.

6. Repeat steps 3, 4, and 5 with the remaining dough till all the cutouts are spaced out on the new cookie sheet. If you can't fit all of them on one sheet, they can be baked in two batches.

7. Using the smaller cookie cutter, cut out the centers of half of the cookies and carefully remove the centers using a small, sharp knife. Bake the cookies for 10 to 12 minutes or till golden and browned on the edges. Remove from the oven, transfer to a cooling rack, and let cool completely.

8. Spread about 1 tablespoon of jam on each cookie without a center cutout and top each one with its cutout partner. If desired, dust with powdered sugar. Serve immediately.

9. The filled cookies will soften if stored. They are best when assembled the day of serving.

Ladyfingers

These biscuit sponge cookies are used for making Tiramisù (page 159), but they are delicious by themselves dipped in coffee as well.

INGREDIENTS

½ cup (100 g) firmly packed maple sugar

1¼ cups (130 g) arrowroot flour

¼ cup (30 g) almond flour

6 large eggs, room temperature, separated

1 teaspoon vanilla extract

¼ teaspoon cream of tartar

Powdered sugar (see page 33), for dusting (optional)

SPECIAL EQUIPMENT

Large pastry bag fitted with a ½-inch (1.25-cm) round tip

YIELD

About thirty 4-inch (10-cm) ladyfingers

METHOD

1. Preheat the oven to 400°F (205°C). Line two large cookie sheets with parchment paper.

2. Pulse the sugar a few times in a small spice/coffee grinder or blender. This will help it dissolve more easily into the eggs. Combine the flours in a bowl, then sift to remove any lumps and set aside.

3. In a medium-sized bowl or the bowl of a stand mixer fitted with a whisk attachment, beat the egg yolks and vanilla on high speed for about 8 minutes or till thick, pale ribbons form. Transfer to a clean bowl.

4. Thoroughly clean the bowl and whisk attachment to remove all traces of grease, then dry completely. Whip the egg whites on medium speed till frothy, add the cream of tartar, and continue beating till soft peaks form. With the mixer running, add the pulsed sugar in a slow, steady stream, then beat on high speed till stiff (but not dry) peaks form. Quickly scrape the beaten egg yolks into the meringue and fold gently with a rubber spatula till only a few streaks of yellow remain. Sift the flour mixture over the eggs and gently fold together till just combined with no lumps. Take care not to deflate the batter too much.

5. Transfer the batter to the pastry bag and pipe into 4-inch (10-cm)-long fingerlike logs. Once piped, dust with powdered sugar and let sit to absorb for a few minutes, then dust once more. The powdered sugar can be omitted; the cookies just won't have the traditional crusted coating.

6. Bake for 8 to 10 minutes or till the tops are slightly golden and spring back when gently pressed.

7. Remove from the oven and let cool slightly before transferring to a cooling rack. Store in an airtight container for up to 1 day.

Maple Candied Bacon Blondies

INGREDIENTS

½ cup (90 g) palm shortening or ghee

2¼ cups (225 g) almond flour

1 cup (200 g) firmly packed maple sugar

¼ teaspoon baking soda

¼ teaspoon salt

2 large eggs

1 tablespoon vanilla extract

8 slices candied bacon (page 93)

¼ cup (25 g) pecans, finely chopped

YIELD

Sixteen 2-inch blondies

METHOD

1. Preheat the oven to 375°F (190°C). Grease an 8-inch (20-cm) square cake/brownie pan and line it with parchment paper. Leave flaps on two sides of the pan for easy removal of the blondies.

2. In a small saucepan over medium heat, melt the shortening just till it becomes liquid. Set aside to cool.

3. In a large bowl, whisk together the flour, sugar, baking soda, and salt till blended. In a separate bowl, lightly beat the eggs, vanilla, and melted shortening, then add the egg mixture to the flour mixture and stir till the batter is well combined and there are no lumps.

4. Transfer the batter to the prepared pan. It will be quite thick, so smooth it out as best you can. Break the candied bacon into small pieces, then sprinkle the top of the batter evenly with the candied bacon and pecan pieces.

5. Bake for 22 to 25 minutes or till the blondies are golden and the center springs back when gently pressed. Remove from the oven and let cool in the pan for at least 10 minutes.

6. Run a knife along the outside edge of the blondies, pull up on the paper flaps, and remove from the pan. Cut into squares and serve. The blondies can also be cut in the pan. They store well, covered, at room temperature for about 2 days. They're also delicious chilled.

Chapter 7:

ICE CREAM & FROZEN DESSERTS

If I had to choose a single dessert to represent the idea of a classic, wholesome family, I would undoubtedly pick ice cream. There's something about the romantic simplicity of the 1950s, Norman Rockwell golden era that conjures up ice cream in my mind. To me, sitting around with the people I love while sharing a bowl of ice cream on a hot summer afternoon represents the very essence of what it means to be a family.

Though ice cream is called many different things around the world, what it most often has in common are milk, eggs, cream, and sugar. For this book, however, ice cream comes in dairy- and refined sugar–free varieties, with coconut milk as the base. The sorbets are water-based confections that include fruit and even chocolate and are naturally egg-free.

Vanilla Ice Cream

INGREDIENTS

2 teaspoons powdered gelatin

3 tablespoons cold water

4 egg yolks

⅔ cup (160 ml) maple syrup or honey

3 cups (750 ml/2 [13½-ounce] cans) full-fat coconut milk

2 teaspoons vanilla extract

1 to 2 tablespoons flavored liqueur of choice (optional)

SPECIAL EQUIPMENT

Candy thermometer

Ice cream maker

YIELD

1½ pints (3 cups/710 ml)

METHOD

1. In a small bowl, sprinkle the gelatin over the cold water and allow to soften (bloom) while you prepare the rest of the ingredients. In a large bowl, whisk together the egg yolks and maple syrup.

2. In a medium-sized saucepan over medium heat, bring 1½ cups (375 ml) of the coconut milk just to a boil. Slowly pour the milk into the egg mixture, whisking constantly to prevent the eggs from seizing. Pour the whole mixture back into the saucepan and cook till it reaches 160°F (70°C) on a candy thermometer, or till it thickens to the consistency of heavy cream. This usually takes about 4 minutes. Gently stir the whole time.

3. Remove from the heat and pour the custard through a fine-mesh sieve into a clean bowl. Whisk in the bloomed gelatin till melted, then whisk in the vanilla and liqueur, if using, and the remaining 1½ cups (375 ml) of coconut milk. Cover and chill till very cold.

4. Freeze in an ice cream maker according to the manufacturer's instructions. Enjoy right away as a soft serve, or transfer to a freezer-safe container and freeze for a few hours or till scoopable.

5. The ice cream will keep for about 1 week when stored in an airtight container. Once stored in the freezer, for the best consistency, let it sit out at room temperature till easily scoopable.

Flavor Variations for Vanilla Ice Cream:

Pistachio Ice Cream.

Heat the coconut milk in a saucepan over medium heat, bringing it just to a boil. Remove the pan from the heat and stir in 1 cup (100 g) of pistachio flour. Set aside to steep and cool for about 30 minutes. Strain the milk through a fine-mesh sieve, add a few drops of almond extract, then use this flavored milk in place of the plain coconut milk in the recipe above.

Hazelnut Ice Cream.

Heat the coconut milk in a saucepan over medium heat, bringing it just to a boil. Remove the pan from the heat and stir in 1 cup (100 g) of hazelnut flour. Set aside to steep and cool for about 30 minutes. Strain the milk through a fine-mesh sieve, then use this flavored milk in place of the plain coconut milk in the recipe above.

Strawberry Ice Cream

INGREDIENTS

1 pound (455 g) fresh strawberries

⅔ cup (160 ml) maple syrup or honey

1 teaspoon lemon juice

Pinch of salt

1½ teaspoons powdered gelatin

3 tablespoons water

2 cups (475 ml) full-fat coconut milk

SPECIAL EQUIPMENT

Ice cream maker

YIELD

About 1 quart (4 cups/1 L)

METHOD

1. Wash, hull, and cut the strawberries in half. Place them in a large bowl and coarsely mash them together with the maple syrup, lemon juice, and salt. Let sit for about 10 minutes, stirring occasionally.

2. Sprinkle the gelatin over the water in a small microwaveable bowl and leave to bloom for at least 5 minutes.

3. Pour the macerated strawberry mixture and the coconut milk into a blender and purée till smooth.

4. Gradually heat the gelatin mixture in the microwave in short bursts till the gelatin has melted. Do not let it boil. Stir the melted gelatin into the strawberry mixture till well combined. Chill till very cold.

5. Freeze in an ice cream maker according to the manufacturer's instructions. Enjoy right away as a soft serve, or transfer to a freezer-safe container and freeze for a few hours or till scoopable.

6. The ice cream will keep for about 1 week when stored in an airtight container. Once stored in the freezer, for the best consistency, let it sit out at room temperature till easily scoopable.

Mixed Berry Sorbet

When making this recipe, feel free to experiment with your favorite combinations rather than sticking to the berry medley suggested below. Different combinations and ratios of berries will create varying colors and flavor profiles.

INGREDIENTS

1 pound (455 g) fresh or frozen mixed blueberries, blackberries, and raspberries

⅔ cup (160 ml) maple syrup or honey

1½ cups (375 ml) water

Juice of 1 small lemon

Grated zest of 1 small lemon

SPECIAL EQUIPMENT

Ice cream maker

YIELD

1½ pints (3 cups/710 ml)

METHOD

1. If using fresh berries, rinse and remove any stems or debris. In a medium-sized saucepan, bring the berries, maple syrup, water, and lemon juice to a boil over medium-high heat. Reduce the heat to low and simmer for 10 minutes. Remove from the heat and let cool to room temperature.

2. In a blender, purée the berry mixture with the lemon zest till smooth, then strain through a fine-mesh sieve. Chill till very cold.

3. Freeze in an ice cream maker according to the manufacturer's instructions. Enjoy right away as a soft serve, or transfer to a freezer-safe container and freeze for a few hours or till scoopable.

4. The sorbet will keep for about 1 week when stored in an airtight container. Once stored in the freezer, for the best consistency, let it sit out at room temperature till easily scoopable.

VARIATION: SWEET WINE AND MIXED BERRY SORBET

Follow the recipe above, but replace up to half of the water with a sweet red wine like Madeira.

Chocolate Sorbet

INGREDIENTS

2¼ cups (540 ml) water

¾ cup (180 ml) maple syrup

¾ cup (75 g) cocoa powder

Pinch of salt

6 ounces (170 g) bittersweet chocolate, finely chopped

½ teaspoon vanilla extract

SPECIAL EQUIPMENT

Ice cream maker

YIELD

1 quart (4 cups/1 L)

METHOD

1. In a large saucepan, whisk together 1½ cups (360 ml) of the water with the maple syrup, cocoa, and salt. Bring the mixture to a boil, stirring often. Once it comes to a boil, continue boiling for another 30 seconds. Remove from the heat and add the chocolate, stirring till melted. Stir in the vanilla and remaining ¾ cup (180 ml) of water. Pour the mixture into a blender and blend for about 10 seconds. Chill till very cold.

2. Freeze in an ice cream maker according to the manufacturer's instructions. Enjoy right away as a soft serve, or transfer to a freezer-safe container and freeze for a few hours or till scoopable.

3. The sorbet will keep for about 1 week when stored in an airtight container. Once stored in the freezer, for the best consistency, let it sit out at room temperature till easily scoopable.

VARIATION: MOCHA SORBET

Follow the recipe above, but replace some of the water with espresso or strong brewed coffee.

Lemon Curd Ice Cream

INGREDIENTS

1 recipe Lemon Curd (page 52),
still warm

1⅔ cups (400 ml) full-
fat coconut milk (from 1
[13½-ounce] can)

Grated zest of 1 small lemon

SPECIAL EQUIPMENT

Ice cream maker

YIELD

1½ pints (3 cups/710 ml)

METHOD

1. Make the lemon curd. While it is still warm, whisk in the coconut milk till well combined. Chill the mixture till very cold.

2. Freeze in an ice cream maker according to the manufacturer's instructions. Enjoy right away as a soft serve, or transfer to a freezer-safe container and freeze for a few hours or till scoopable.

3. The ice cream will keep for about 1 week when stored in an airtight container. Once stored in the freezer, for the best consistency, let it sit out at room temperature till easily scoopable.

Rocky Road Sorbet

INGREDIENTS

½ recipe marshmallow crème for Classic Marshmallows (page 222)

1 recipe Chocolate Sorbet base (page 195), chilled

¼ cup (25 g) chopped toasted pecans or walnuts

SPECIAL EQUIPMENT

Candy thermometer

Ice cream maker

YIELD

1 quart (4 cups/1 L)

METHOD

1. A few hours or the night before you make the sorbet, make the marshmallow crème: Prepare an 8-inch (20-cm) square pan or other pan of similar size, following the instructions in step 1 of the Classic Marshmallows recipe, making sure to dust the bottom of the pan with arrowroot flour. Once the crème is ready, spread it in the prepared pan and dust the top with a light layer of arrowroot flour. Leave to cure (set) for at least 4 hours or overnight, covered with a flour sack towel.

2. Freeze the chilled chocolate sorbet base in an ice cream maker according to the manufacturer's instructions.

3. While the sorbet is churning, cut the marshmallows into small pieces. When the sorbet is almost done, sprinkle in the nuts and as many marshmallows as you like. You probably won't use all of them (see page 222 for information on storing leftover marshmallows). Continue churning till the add-ins are evenly mixed into the sorbet. If the ice cream maker bogs down, scoop the sorbet into a bowl and stir in the add-ins by hand.

4. Enjoy right away as a soft serve, or transfer to a freezer-safe container and freeze for a few hours or till scoopable.

5. The sorbet will keep for about 1 week when stored in an airtight container. Once stored in the freezer, for the best consistency, let it sit out at room temperature till easily scoopable.

Strawberry Lemonade Baked Alaska

This recipe uses my coconut flour–based vanilla cake batter, making this dessert nut-free, but you can use any cake and ice cream combination you can dream up! For photo instructions, see pages 282–283.

INGREDIENTS

1 recipe Nut-Free Vanilla Cake batter (page 134)

1 recipe Lemon Curd Ice Cream (page 197)

1 recipe Strawberry Ice Cream (page 193)

1 recipe Swiss Meringue (page 57)

SPECIAL EQUIPMENT

15 by 10-inch (38 by 25-cm) jelly roll pan

Ceramic or stainless-steel bowl that holds about 5 cups (1.2 L) of liquid, with a 7-inch (18-cm) diameter rim, to serve as the mold for the cake

Kitchen torch

SERVES

8 to 10

METHOD

1. Preheat the oven to 350°F (177°C). Grease a 15 by 10-inch (38 by 25-cm) jelly roll pan and line it with parchment paper.

2. Prepare the cake batter, then pour it into the prepared pan and spread till smooth. Bake for about 12 minutes, or till the cake springs back when pressed. While the cake is baking, remove the lemon curd ice cream from the freezer to soften. Let the cake cool slightly, then remove from the pan and let cool on a wire rack. Cut the cake to fit the inside rim of the bowl you're using as the mold. (There will be cake left over.)

3. Assemble the cake: To make the ice cream cake easier to remove once frozen, line the bowl with plastic wrap, letting it hang over the edges. Scoop about ½ cup (120 ml) of softened lemon curd ice cream into the bowl. Smooth the top, then put the bowl and the remaining lemon curd ice cream in the freezer for about 30 minutes. Meanwhile, soften the strawberry ice cream, then scoop about 2 cups (475 ml) on top of the lemon curd ice cream in the bowl. Smooth the top and put it back in the freezer for another 30 minutes. Soften the lemon curd ice cream again and scoop about 2 more cups (475 ml) on top of the strawberry ice cream. Fit the trimmed cake layer on top, making sure that it sticks to the ice cream. Cover with plastic wrap and freeze for about 6 hours, till frozen solid.

4. Remove the cake from the bowl by slightly warming the outside of the bowl with a hot wet towel, then pulling on the overhanging plastic wrap. If the ice cream has become soft, wrap up the cake and put it back in the freezer for a few hours or till ready to use. The cake needs to be frozen solid; otherwise, the meringue won't stick to the cake.

5. Just before serving the cake, make the meringue. Decoratively cover the cake with the meringue, then use a kitchen torch to brown the outside of the meringue. Serve immediately.

Strawberry, Pistachio, & Vanilla Layered Ice Cream Cake

This triple-layered ice cream cake is easy to make, but it may take a few days to prepare the ice creams, depending on what kind of ice cream maker you have.

INGREDIENTS

1 Chocolate Joconde Cake (page 149)

1 recipe Strawberry Ice Cream (page 193)

1 recipe Pistachio Ice Cream (page 192)

1 recipe Vanilla Ice Cream (page 192)

1 (6-ounce/170-g) bar bittersweet chocolate or 6 ounces (170 g) bittersweet chocolate chips

¼ cup (25 g) chopped raw pistachio meats, for garnish

A few fresh strawberries, hulled, for garnish

SPECIAL EQUIPMENT

9 by 5-inch (23 by 12.75-cm) or 10 by 4-inch (25 by 10-cm) loaf pan with a capacity of a little more than 6 cups (1.4 L), to serve as the mold for the cake

SERVES

8 to 10

METHOD

1. Make the joconde cake the day you assemble the ice cream cake. Cut it to fit the inside rim of the loaf pan you're using as the mold. (There will be cake left over.) Cover with a tea towel or plastic wrap and set aside.

2. Assemble the cake: To make the ice cream cake easier to remove once frozen, line the mold with plastic wrap, letting it hang over the edges. Let the strawberry ice cream sit out till it has the consistency of soft serve. Scoop about 2 cups (475 ml) into the mold. (There will be ice cream left over.) Smooth the top with a spatula, then put the mold in the freezer for about 30 minutes. Meanwhile, soften the pistachio ice cream in the same way. Scoop about 2 cups on top of the strawberry ice cream in the mold, smooth the top, and put it back in freezer for another 30 minutes. Soften the vanilla ice cream and scoop about 2 cups (475 ml) on top of the pistachio ice cream. Place the trimmed cake layer on top, making sure that it sticks to the ice cream. Cover with plastic wrap and freeze for about 6 hours, till frozen solid.

3. Remove the cake from the mold by slightly warming the outside of the mold with a hot, wet towel and pulling on the overhanging plastic wrap. To remove any wrinkles in the cake from the plastic wrap, simply trim the sides with a hot knife. Put the cake back in the freezer till the outside is frozen solid or you are ready to serve it. This is important so that the chocolate coating sticks and doesn't slide off.

4. To finish the cake, heat the chocolate in a double broiler till just melted. Remove from the heat and let cool to lukewarm. The chocolate needs to be cool enough not to melt the cake but warm enough to be pourable. Pour the chocolate toward the center of the cake and use a spatula to spread it toward the edges, letting some of it drizzle down over the sides. It will harden quickly. Sprinkle the top with the chopped pistachios and a few strawberries. Slice and serve.

Berry Sorbet Swiss Roll Cake

Like the other ice cream cakes in this chapter, this recipe is very flexible. You can use any of the joconde cakes and ice creams to make endless varieties of ice cream cake rolls.

INGREDIENTS

1 Joconde Cake (pages 148–149)

1 recipe Mixed Berry Sorbet (page 194)

Powdered sugar (see page 33), for dusting (optional)

SERVES

8 to 10

METHOD

1. After removing the cake from the oven, form it into a roll, following step 8 in the Joconde Cake recipe, and allow it to cool completely. (It must be completely cool or the sorbet will melt too much when spread over it.)

2. While the cake is cooling, prepare the sorbet and churn in an ice cream maker till thick and frozen. (If you made the sorbet ahead of time, set it out on the counter to let it soften to soft-serve consistency.)

3. Unroll the cake and immediately spread the sorbet over the cake, making it about ¼ inch (6 mm) thick. Leave a small border around the whole cake to make it easier to roll up. Now roll it up just like you did the first time, only without the flour sack towel. Transfer the cake to a cookie sheet and place in the freezer till firm enough to wrap in plastic wrap or freezer paper.

4. Continue to freeze till solid and ready to slice and serve. Before serving, dust with powdered sugar if desired.

Linzer Cookie Ice Cream Sandwiches

INGREDIENTS

1 recipe Linzer Cookies
(page 183)

1 recipe Mixed Berry Sorbet
(page 194), made with all
raspberries

SPECIAL EQUIPMENT

*1 (3-inch/7.5-cm) round or
scalloped cookie cutter*

YIELD

8 ice cream sandwiches

METHOD

1. Prepare the cookies as instructed, minus the
raspberry jam.

2. Prepare the sorbet, then transfer it to a 9 by 13-inch/
23 by 33-cm (3-quart/3-L) baking dish. Smooth it out
as evenly as possible, cover, and freeze till firm.

3. When ready to assemble the ice cream sandwiches,
remove the sorbet from the freezer and, using the
same cutter you used for the cookies, cut the sorbet
into shapes. If needed, dip the cutter in hot water
before cutting.

4. Place each sorbet piece on a cookie, lining it up so
that the edges have a clean look. Place another cookie
on top, then transfer the sandwiches to a cookie sheet
and freeze again, uncovered, till firm. Transfer to a
covered container and store for up to 1 week.

Waffle Cones

These nut flour–based waffle cones are made on a standard 4½-inch (11.5-cm) pizzelle maker and rolled into the traditional waffle cone shape.

INGREDIENTS

2 tablespoons palm shortening or ghee

1 large egg

1 large egg white

¼ cup (50 g) firmly packed maple sugar

2 teaspoons vanilla extract

¾ cup (75 g) almond flour

3 tablespoons arrowroot flour

¼ teaspoon salt

SPECIAL EQUIPMENT

Pizzelle maker with 4½-inch (11.5-cm) molds or standard-size waffle cone maker

Cone-shaped roller (helpful but not necessary)

YIELD

About 10 small pizzelle-sized cones

METHOD

1. Preheat a pizzelle maker or waffle cone maker.

2. Melt the shortening in a small saucepan and allow to cool slightly.

3. In a medium-sized bowl, whisk together the whole egg, egg white, sugar, vanilla, and melted shortening till smooth. Add the flours and salt and whisk till smooth again. Let the batter rest for about 5 minutes.

4. Scoop 1 tablespoon of the batter onto the center of the pizzelle/waffle cone maker. Close the lid and cook for 30 to 60 seconds or till the cookie is done.

5. Place the cookie on the countertop and immediately shape it with a cone roller or by hand. Hold the cone on the roller till it feels like it will hold its shape. It will set quickly as it cools. If it doesn't crisp up once cooled, then you know it needs to cook longer. If your machine browns the cookie more on one side than the other, flip the cookie halfway through the cooking time for more even browning.

6. The cones are best eaten the day they are made.

Flavor Variations for Waffle Cones:

Hazelnut Waffle Cones.
Replace the almond flour with an equal amount of hazelnut flour.

Chocolate Waffle Cones.
Use just 1 tablespoon of arrowroot flour and add 2 tablespoons of cocoa powder.

Nut-Free Vanilla Waffle Cones

These nut-free waffle cones can be used for any of the recipes that call for waffle cones or waffle cone batter.

INGREDIENTS

¼ cup (45 g) palm shortening or ghee

3 tablespoons coconut flour

3 tablespoons arrowroot flour

1 large egg

1 large egg white

¼ cup (60 ml) maple syrup

1 tablespoon vanilla extract

Pinch of salt

SPECIAL EQUIPMENT

Pizzelle maker with 4½-inch (11.5-cm) molds or standard-size waffle cone maker

Cone-shaped roller (helpful but not necessary)

YIELD

About 10 small pizzelle-sized cones

METHOD

1. Preheat a pizzelle maker or waffle cone maker.

2. Melt the shortening in a small saucepan and allow to cool slightly.

3. In a medium-sized bowl, whisk together the flours, whole egg, egg white, maple syrup, vanilla, salt, and melted shortening till smooth. Let the batter rest for about 5 minutes.

4. Scoop 1 tablespoon of the batter onto the center of the pizzelle/waffle cone maker. Close the lid and cook for 30 to 60 seconds or till the cookie is done.

5. Place the cookie on the countertop and immediately shape it with a cone roller or by hand. Hold the cone on the roller till it feels like it will hold its shape. It will set quickly as it cools. If it doesn't crisp up once cooled, then you know it needs to cook longer. If your machine browns the cookie more on one side than the other, flip the cookie halfway through the cooking time for more even browning.

6. The cones are best eaten the day they are made.

ROLLED (PIZZELLE) CANNOLI

These delicious cookies are filled with coconut whipped cream and frozen for an easy frozen treat. Be creative and fill them with whatever you like.

Cream-Filled Cannoli with Pistachios

INGREDIENTS

1 recipe Waffle Cone batter (page 212)

1 recipe Sweetened Whipped Cream (page 48)

½ cup (50 g) chopped pistachio meats, raw or toasted

SPECIAL EQUIPMENT

Pizzelle maker with 4½-inch (11.5-cm) molds

Cylinder-shaped cannoli roller

Pastry bag fitted with a ½-inch (1.25-cm) star tip (optional)

YIELD

About 10 cannoli

METHOD

1. Prepare the waffle cone batter and cook as instructed in the recipe, but instead of using a cone-shaped roller, use a cylinder-shaped cannoli roller to form tubes (or just roll by hand). Hold the cookie on the roller till it feels like it will hold its shape. Remove, then let cool completely.

2. Use the pastry bag or a spoon to generously fill each cookie with the whipped cream. Then, one at a time, dip both ends in the pistachios. Press the nuts in gently to secure.

3. Place on a cookie sheet and freeze for at least 1 hour. Once frozen, they can be transferred to a sealed container and kept frozen for several days. Serve straight from the freezer.

Double Chocolate Cannoli

INGREDIENTS

1 recipe Chocolate Waffle Cone batter (page 212)

1 recipe Chocolate Whipped Cream (page 48)

½ cup (120 g) mini chocolate chips

SPECIAL EQUIPMENT

Pizzelle maker with 4½-inch (11.5-cm) molds

Cylinder-shaped cannoli roller

Pastry bag fitted with a ½-inch (1.25-cm) star tip (optional)

YIELD

About 10 cannoli

METHOD

1. Prepare the waffle cone batter and cook as instructed in the recipe, but instead of using a cone-shaped roller, use a cylinder-shaped cannoli roller to form tubes (or just roll by hand). Hold the cookie on the roller till it feels like it will hold its shape. Remove, then let cool completely.

2. Use the pastry bag or a spoon to generously fill each cookie with the whipped cream. Then, one at a time, dip both ends in the mini chocolate chips. Press the chocolate chips in gently to secure.

3. Place on a cookie sheet and freeze for at least 1 hour. Once frozen, they can be transferred to a sealed container and kept frozen for several days. Serve straight from the freezer.

Pistachio Drumsticks

You can prepare the pistachio ice cream ahead of time, but the waffle cones should be made the same day you assemble the drumsticks, as they are best the day they are made.

INGREDIENTS

1 recipe Pistachio Ice Cream (page 192)

6 Waffle Cones (page 212)

1 cup (5 ounces/140 g) whole raw pistachio meats

10 to 12 ounces (285 to 340 g) bittersweet chocolate, chopped

SPECIAL EQUIPMENT

Egg carton waffle cone stand (see page 284 for instructions)

YIELD

6 drumsticks

METHOD

1. You will need something that allows the cones to stand upright to freeze and set. I like to take an old egg carton, turn it upside down so that the molded part is facing up, and then, using a sharp serrated knife, cut about ¼ inch (6 mm) off the tips. You may have to shave off a little more to get a good fit. This setup also works well for letting the cones set after rolling them. See pages 284–285 for photo instructions.

2. You want the ice cream to be soft enough to scoop, but firm enough to hold a scooped shape. If you have made the ice cream ahead of time, allow it to sit out at room temperature till it's soft enough to make nice round scoops. You will need about ½ cup (120 ml) of ice cream to fill each cone. Working quickly, fill each cone with 2 tablespoons of softened ice cream, gently pressing it down into the cone. Then scoop out a nice-sized ball of ice cream, pressing it on top of the cone. Set the cones in the egg carton stand and place in the freezer for 1 to 2 hours or till frozen solid.

3. When the cones are ready, coarsely chop the pistachios and place them in a shallow bowl. Put the chocolate in a heatproof bowl over a pot of simmering water. Heat till just melted, then remove the bowl from the heat. If the chocolate gets thick again, just place the bowl back over the water till it is workable.

4. Take the cones out of the freezer one by one and dip them in the chocolate, using a spoon to help coat all the edges. Immediately sprinkle and press the outside with the chopped pistachios. You must work quickly because the chocolate will begin to harden fast. Place the drumstick back in the freezer and repeat with the next cone till they are all coated. Freeze till firm.

5. Once the dipped and rolled cones have set, they can be stored in a large freezer bag or sealed container for up to 1 week. Serve straight from the freezer.

Chapter 8:

MARSHMALLOWS

For many people, the notion of eating marshmallows is inseparably linked to the idea of making s'mores. While this is definitely a wonderful use for them, for me marshmallows have always been less about how they are used and more about how they make people feel.

Marshmallows bring joy. They are playful and fascinating, and their billowy lightness is reflected in the way we feel when we eat them. They bring out the child in everyone, and I've never seen them fail to put a smile on someone's face.

Classic Marshmallows

The marshmallows in this chapter can be made with all honey or all maple syrup; however, I find that a combination of the two yields the best flavor, volume, and texture. For photo instructions, see pages 286–287.

INGREDIENTS

¼ cup (30 g) arrowroot flour, for dusting

1 cup (240 ml) water

2½ tablespoons powdered gelatin

¾ cup (180 ml) maple syrup

½ cup (120 ml) honey

Pinch of salt

2 teaspoons vanilla extract

SPECIAL EQUIPMENT

Candy thermometer

Offset spatula

YIELD

Twenty-five 1½-inch (4-cm) square marshmallows

METHOD

1. Grease an 8-inch (20-cm) square pan and line it with parchment paper, leaving some length on both sides to use as handles when removing the finished marshmallows. Dust the parchment with a light layer of arrowroot flour.

2. Place ½ cup (120 ml) of the water in the bowl of a stand mixer, then sprinkle the gelatin evenly over the water. Stir to combine if needed. Leave the gelatin to bloom while you prepare the rest of the recipe.

3. Combine the remaining ½ cup (120 ml) of water, maple syrup, and salt in a medium-sized saucepan. Bring the mixture to a boil over medium-high heat (watch closely, as it tends to foam up). Place a candy thermometer in the mixture and continue to boil till it reaches 240°F (114°C). This usually takes 12 to 15 minutes after the first boil, but times can vary.

4. Secure the bowl to the stand mixer fitted with the whisk attachment. With the mixer running at medium-low speed, pour the hot syrup into the bowl in a slow, steady stream. Be sure that it melts all of the gelatin mixture. Try to avoid hitting the whisk or you will fling syrup all over the bowl. Turn the mixer up to high speed and continue beating till the mixture nearly triples in volume and the marshmallow crème is just cool to the touch (this usually takes 5 to 7 minutes, or longer if using a hand mixer). To check whether the marshmallow crème is ready, stop the mixer and lift up the whisk. The mixture should fall slowly off the whisk, like lava, before melting back into itself. Beat in the vanilla till just combined.

5. Transfer the marshmallow crème to the prepared pan, using a rubber spatula to clean the bowl. The crème should fill the pan about two-thirds full. Working quickly, smooth the top with an offset spatula, then dust with a light layer of arrowroot flour.

6. Leave to cure (set), uncovered, for at least 4 hours. If leaving overnight, cover the pan with a light flour sack towel.

7. Lift the marshmallows from the pan and cut into 1½-inch (4-cm) squares. Lightly toss with more arrowroot flour. I like to place the coated marshmallows in a fine-mesh strainer and shake off any excess coating for a smooth finish.

8. Store in an airtight container for up to 1 day, or freeze for 1 month. Let thaw to room temperature before serving.

Chocolate Marshmallows

Chocolate marshmallows have slightly less volume than the other varieties due to the weight of the cocoa.

INGREDIENTS

For the dusting mixture:

1 tablespoon cocoa powder

¼ cup (30 g) arrowroot flour

1 cup (240 ml) plus 3 tablespoons water

¼ cup (25 g) cocoa powder

2½ tablespoons powdered gelatin

¾ cup (180 ml) maple syrup

½ cup (120 ml) honey

¼ teaspoon salt

1 teaspoon vanilla extract

SPECIAL EQUIPMENT

Candy thermometer

Offset spatula

YIELD

Twenty-five 1½-inch (4-cm) square marshmallows

METHOD

1. Grease an 8-inch (20-cm) square pan and line it with parchment paper, leaving some length on both sides to use as handles when removing the finished marshmallows.

2. Make the dusting mixture: In a small bowl, combine 1 tablespoon of cocoa with the arrowroot flour. Lightly grease the parchment paper and sprinkle with a light layer of the dusting mixture.

3. In another bowl, whisk together 3 tablespoons of the water with ¼ cup (25 g) cocoa till it forms a paste. Add ½ cup (120 ml) of the water to the bowl of a stand mixer, then sprinkle the gelatin evenly over the water. Add the cocoa paste and mix to combine. Leave the gelatin mixture to bloom while you prepare the rest of the recipe.

4. Continue with steps 3–8 of the Classic Marshmallows recipe on page 222.

NOTE

If you desire a sweet dusting powder, replace 2 tablespoons of the arrowroot flour in the dusting mixture with 2 tablespoons of powdered sugar (see page 33).

Raspberry Marshmallows

INGREDIENTS

¼ cup (30 g) arrowroot flour, for dusting

1 tablespoon lemon juice

3 tablespoons raspberry powder (see page 37)

1 cup (240 ml) water

2½ tablespoons powdered gelatin

¾ cup (180 ml) maple syrup

½ cup (120 ml) honey

¼ teaspoon salt

SPECIAL EQUIPMENT

Candy thermometer

Offset spatula

YIELD

Twenty-five 1½-inch (4-cm) square marshmallows

METHOD

1. Grease an 8-inch (20-cm) square pan and line it with parchment paper, leaving some length on both sides to use as handles when removing the finished marshmallows. Dust the parchment with a light layer of arrowroot flour.

2. In another bowl, whisk together the lemon juice and raspberry powder till it forms a paste. Add ½ cup (120 ml) of the water to the bowl of a stand mixer, then sprinkle the gelatin evenly over the water. Add the raspberry paste and mix to combine. Leave the gelatin mixture to bloom while you prepare the rest of the recipe.

3. Continue with steps 3–8 of the Classic Marshmallows recipe on page 222.

NOTE

If you desire a sweet dusting powder, replace 2 tablespoons of the arrowroot flour with 2 tablespoons of powdered sugar (see page 33).

Matcha Green Tea Marshmallows

INGREDIENTS

For the dusting mixture:

1 teaspoon matcha green tea powder

¼ cup (30 g) arrowroot flour

1 cup (240 ml) plus 1 tablespoon water

1 tablespoon matcha green tea powder

2½ tablespoons powdered gelatin

¾ cup (180 ml) maple syrup

½ cup (120 ml) honey

¼ teaspoon salt

SPECIAL EQUIPMENT

Candy thermometer

Offset spatula

YIELD

Twenty-five 1½-inch (4-cm) square marshmallows

METHOD

1. Grease an 8-inch (20-cm) square pan and line it with parchment paper, leaving some length on both sides to use as handles when removing the finished marshmallows.

2. Make the dusting mixture: In a small bowl, combine 1 teaspoon of green tea powder with the arrowroot flour. Lightly grease the parchment paper and sprinkle with a light layer of the dusting mixture.

3. In another bowl, whisk together 1 tablespoon of the water with 1 tablespoon of green tea powder till it forms a paste. Add ½ cup (120 ml) of the water to the bowl of a stand mixer, then sprinkle the gelatin evenly over the water. Add the green tea paste and mix to combine. Leave the gelatin mixture to bloom while you prepare the rest of the recipe.

4. Continue with steps 3–8 of the Classic Marshmallows recipe on page 222.

NOTE

If you desire a sweet dusting powder, replace 2 tablespoons of the arrowroot flour in the dusting mixture with 2 tablespoons of powdered sugar (see page 33).

Earl Grey Tea Marshmallows

INGREDIENTS

¼ cup (30 g) arrowroot flour, for dusting

1 cup (240 ml) water

6 bags (or 2 tablespoons loose-leaf) Earl Grey tea

2½ tablespoons powdered gelatin

¾ cup (180 ml) maple syrup

½ cup (120 ml) honey

¼ teaspoon salt

SPECIAL EQUIPMENT

Candy thermometer

Offset spatula

YIELD

Twenty-five 1-inch (4-cm) square marshmallows

METHOD

1. Grease an 8-inch (20-cm) square pan and line it with parchment paper, leaving some length on both sides to use as handles when removing the finished marshmallows. Dust the parchment with a light layer of arrowroot flour.

2. In a small saucepan, bring ½ cup (120 ml) of the water just to a boil. If using loose-leaf tea, put the tea leaves in a tea bag. Steep the tea in the water for 4 minutes, remove the bags, and squeeze out as much tea as possible. Measure the tea; if you don't have ½ cup (120 ml) of liquid left, add a little water to make up the difference. Chill till cold.

3. Once chilled, pour the tea into the bowl of a stand mixer, then sprinkle the gelatin evenly over the tea. Leave the gelatin mixture to bloom while you prepare the rest of the recipe.

4. Continue with steps 3–8 of the Classic Marshmallows recipe on page 222.

NOTE

If you desire a sweet dusting powder, replace 2 tablespoons of the arrowroot flour with 2 tablespoons of powdered sugar (see page 33).

Raspberry Neapolitan Marshmallows

INGREDIENTS

¼ cup (30 g) arrowroot flour, for dusting

1 recipe marshmallow crème for Raspberry Marshmallows (page 227)

1 recipe marshmallow crème for Chocolate Marshmallows (page 225)

1 recipe marshmallow crème for Classic Marshmallows (page 222)

SPECIAL EQUIPMENT

Candy thermometer

Offset spatula

YIELD

Twenty-four 2-inch (5-cm) square marshmallows

METHOD

1. Grease a 9 by 13-inch (23 by 33-cm) baking dish and line it with parchment paper, leaving some length on both sides to use as handles when removing the finished marshmallows. Dust the parchment with a light layer of arrowroot flour.

2. To assemble: Prepare the raspberry marshmallow crème as instructed and transfer to the prepared dish. Using a spatula, smooth the layer as much as possible. Leave to set while you prepare the chocolate marshmallow crème. When ready, spread it on top of the raspberry crème, again smoothing the layer as much as possible. Allow to set while you prepare the vanilla marshmallow crème. When ready, spread it on top of the chocolate crème. Smooth the top with an offset spatula and sprinkle with a layer of arrowroot flour.

3. Leave to cure (set), uncovered, for at least 4 hours. If leaving overnight, lightly cover with a flour sack towel.

4. Lift the marshmallows from the pan and cut into 2-inch (5-cm) squares. Lightly toss with more arrowroot flour. I like to place the coated marshmallows in a fine-mesh strainer and shake off any excess coating and let the colors shine through.

5. Store in an airtight container for up to 1 day, or freeze for 1 month. Let thaw to room temperature before serving.

Gingerbread Spice Marshmallows

INGREDIENTS

For the dusting mixture:

¼ cup (30 g) arrowroot flour

1 teaspoon ground cinnamon

½ teaspoon ginger powder

Pinch of ground cloves

1 teaspoon ginger powder

1 teaspoon ground cinnamon

¼ teaspoon ground cloves

Pinch of ground nutmeg

1 recipe marshmallow crème for Classic Marshmallows (page 222)

1 tablespoon molasses

SPECIAL EQUIPMENT

Candy thermometer

Offset spatula

YIELD

Twenty-five 1½-inch (4-cm) square marshmallows

METHOD

1. Grease an 8-inch (20-cm) square pan and line it with parchment paper, leaving some length on both sides to use as handles when removing the finished marshmallows.

2. Make the dusting mixture: In a small bowl, combine the arrowroot flour and spices for the coating, mixing well. In another small bowl, combine the additional ginger, cinnamon, cloves, and nutmeg. Lightly grease the parchment paper and sprinkle with a light layer of the dusting mixture.

3. Prepare the marshmallow crème according to the Classic Marshmallows recipe, but add the spice mixture and molasses along with the vanilla in step 4. Pour into the prepared pan and smooth with an offset spatula. Dust the top with a layer of the spiced coating.

4. Leave to cure (set), uncovered, for at least 4 hours. If leaving overnight, lightly cover with a flour sack towel.

5. Lift the marshmallows from the pan and cut into 1½-inch (4-cm) squares, adding more dusting mixture while cutting to reduce the stickiness. Lightly toss the cut marshmallows in the remaining dusting mixture. I like to place the coated marshmallows in a fine-mesh strainer and shake off any excess coating for a smooth finish.

6. Store in an airtight container for up to 1 day, or freeze for 1 month. Let thaw to room temperature before serving. To make a Ginger Snap sandwich as pictured, lightly roast the marshmallow and serve between two Ginger Snap cookies (page 172).

Candied Bacon Marshmallows

INGREDIENTS

8 slices candied bacon (page 93)

¼ cup (30 g) arrowroot flour, for dusting

1 recipe marshmallow crème for Classic Marshmallows (page 222)

SPECIAL EQUIPMENT

Candy thermometer

Offset spatula

YIELD

Twenty-five 1½-inch (4-cm) square marshmallows

METHOD

1. Make the candied bacon and break or chop it into small bits.

2. Grease an 8-inch (20-cm) square pan and line it with parchment paper, leaving some length on both sides to use as handles when removing the finished marshmallows. Dust the parchment with a light layer of arrowroot flour.

3. Prepare the marshmallow crème and pour into the prepared pan. Smooth with an offset spatula and sprinkle the candied bacon bits evenly across the top of the marshmallows.

4. Leave to cure (set), uncovered, for at least 4 hours. If leaving overnight, lightly cover with a flour sack towel.

5. Lift the marshmallows from the pan and cut into 1½-inch (4-cm) squares. Lightly toss with more arrowroot flour. I like to place the coated marshmallows in a fine-mesh strainer and shake off any excess coating for a smooth finish.

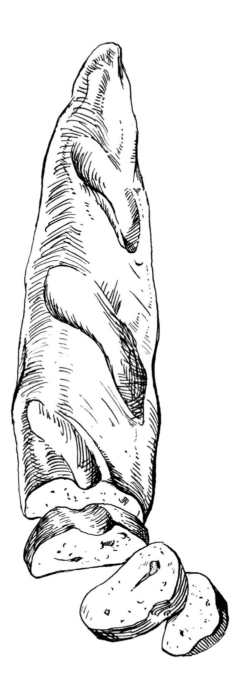

Chapter 9:

SAVORY PASTRIES

It can be easy to overlook savory pastries in all the excitement about beautiful desserts, but they are just as important as their sweet cousins. All the history, depth, culture, and refinement that elevated sweet desserts to their status as the essence of classical patisserie have also been infused into the savory items that evolved alongside them in the cafés and pastry shops of the world. Savory pastries require the exact same spirit of creative, artisanal craftsmanship that sweet pastries do, and that is what gives them their place in this book.

Grissini

Grissini are the long, thin, crispy breadsticks commonly served at cafés in Italy and all over Europe. They can be eaten as snacks or even garnished with things like prosciutto and served as an hors d'oeuvre.

INGREDIENTS

1 recipe Pâte à Choux (page 74)

1 large egg plus 1 tablespoon water, for the egg wash

Coarse salt and/or other toppings, such as poppy seeds or sesame seeds (about ¼ cup)

SPECIAL EQUIPMENT

Large pastry bag fitted with a ¼-inch (6-mm) round tip

YIELD

24 grissini

METHOD

1. Preheat the oven to 400°F (205°C). Grease and line two cookie sheets with parchment paper (the reusable kind works best here, as it wrinkles less). Place a rack in the center position of the oven.

2. Using the pastry bag, pipe the prepared dough into 12-inch (30.5-cm)-long and about ½-inch (1.25-cm)-wide lines on the cookie sheets. They will spread slightly, so space them about 1 inch (2.5 cm) apart. A standard sheet should fit approximately 12 to 15 lines. (See pages 288–289 for photo instructions.)

3. For the best shape, make both ends slightly larger than the rest of the grissini. Keep the piping bag moving at a steady pace, using even pressure to push the dough out. If you have holes because of air bubbles, just fill them in with a small amount of dough. The knobbiness makes them look more rustic anyway.

4. Using a pastry brush, wet the top of each grissini with the egg wash and then sprinkle lightly with coarse salt and/or other toppings.

5. For best results, bake one sheet at a time on the center rack of the oven. Place the second sheet in the freezer till ready to bake. Bake for 18 to 20 minutes for softer grissini or 25 minutes for crispier grissini. (Times will vary depending on thickness.) Do not open the oven door for at least 15 minutes of the baking time, or the grissini could deflate.

NOTE

Instead of baking all of the grissini at once, you can freeze some or all of the piped dough till solid, transfer to a freezer bag for storing, and bake straight from the freezer as needed, just before serving—which I highly recommend, as the grissini are most delicious when warm and fresh.

Italian Pesto Pizza

INGREDIENTS

1 recipe Pâte à Choux (page 74)

For the pesto sauce (dairy- and nut-free):

2 cups (60 g) loosely packed basil leaves

1 large clove garlic

2 tablespoons olive oil

½ teaspoon coarse salt

Toppings:

6 ounces (170 g) aged goat's milk cheddar cheese, shredded (optional)

6 to 8 large-sliced pepperoni

½ small red onion, thinly sliced

A handful of pitted green and/or black olives, thinly sliced

YIELD

One 13-inch (33-cm) round or 15-inch (38-cm) oblong pizza

METHOD

1. Preheat the oven to 400°F (205°C). Line a cookie sheet with parchment paper.

2. Make the crust: Place the prepared dough in the center of the lined cookie sheet. Using the back of a large spoon, spread it out into approximately a 13-inch (33-cm) circle or 15-inch (38-cm) oblong shape. Work the dough from the center outward so that there is a thicker rim of dough around the outside. The center can be quite thin, but not so thin that you can see through to the paper.

3. Bake for 20 minutes, then turn the heat down to 350°F (177°C) and bake for another 15 minutes or till the crust is crispy and puffed. Remove from the oven and let cool (but leave the oven on).

4. While the crust cools, make the pesto: Combine all the pesto ingredients in a food processor and process till smooth. Add more oil as needed to reach the desired consistency. You want it to be spreadable, but not too thin.

5. When ready to assemble the pizza, spread a thin layer of the pesto on the crust. If adding cheese, sprinkle it over the pesto. Arrange the pepperoni, then evenly sprinkle the onion and olives about. Bake for 15 minutes or till the bottom of the crust is crispy. It's normal for the outside of the crust to darken. Remove from the oven and let cool for a few minutes. Slice and serve.

Popovers

Popovers are light, hollow rolls made from an egg batter similar to that of Yorkshire pudding.

INGREDIENTS

3 tablespoons arrowroot flour

2 tablespoons coconut flour

¼ teaspoon salt

4 large eggs, room temperature

¼ cup (60 ml) full-fat coconut milk*

¼ cup (60 ml) water*

1 tablespoon fat of choice, for greasing the pan

Can substitute ½ cup (120 ml) of alternative milk for the water and milk.

SPECIAL EQUIPMENT

Popover pan

YIELD

6 popovers

METHOD

1. Preheat the oven to 450°F (232°C).

2. In a small bowl, combine the flours and salt. In a medium-sized bowl, lightly beat the eggs just to loosen them up, then whisk in the coconut milk, water, and flour mixture. Continue whisking till just smooth.

3. Scoop about ¼ teaspoon to a scant ½ teaspoon of the fat into each well of the popover pan, then place the greased pan in the preheated oven for about 5 minutes, just till the fat starts to smoke. Carefully remove the pan from the oven and quickly pour ¼ cup (60 ml) of the batter into each well.

4. Bake for 15 minutes, then turn the oven temperature down to 350°F (177°C) and bake for another 15 minutes or till the popovers are golden and puffed. Times will vary based on the pan.

Bruschetta Tart

INGREDIENTS

For the bruschetta:

3 tablespoons olive oil

⅓ cup (10 g) loosely packed fresh basil leaves, chopped

1 medium clove garlic, minced

1½ pounds (680 g) Roma tomatoes, diced

Coarse salt and black pepper

1 large clove garlic

1 (9-inch/23-cm) Nut-Free Savory Crust (opposite), prebaked

YIELD

One 9-inch (23-cm) tart

METHOD

1. Make the bruschetta: Combine the olive oil, basil, minced garlic, and tomatoes in a large bowl. Add salt and pepper to taste.

2. When ready to assemble the tart, cut the large garlic clove in half and gently rub it all over the bottom of the crust. Fill the crust with the bruschetta topping. You can use more or less depending on your preference. Serve immediately.

Nut-Free Savory Crust

This is a very delicate crust made with coconut flour. It is called for only once in this book, for the Bruschetta Tart (opposite), but can be used for any recipe that calls for a savory crust.

INGREDIENTS

½ cup (60 g) coconut flour

⅓ cup (40 g) arrowroot flour

Pinch of salt

½ cup (90 g) palm shortening or ghee, softened

2 large eggs, cold

1 tablespoon cold water

YIELD

One 9-inch (23-cm) crust, four 4-inch (10-cm) crusts, five or six 3-inch (7.5-cm) crusts, or 12 mini crusts using a 12-well mini tart pan

METHOD

1. Preheat the oven to 325°F (163°C).

2. In a large bowl, whisk together the flours and salt till blended. Add the remaining ingredients and mix with a wooden spoon till a soft, wet dough has formed. Gather up the dough, wrap in plastic, and chill for about 10 minutes.

3. Press the dough evenly into the pan(s) to a thickness of about ⅛ inch (3 mm). If pressing into several pans, divide the dough into equal portions first.

4. Prick all over with a fork and chill in the freezer for about 10 minutes.

5. Bake for the following times or till golden all over:

   mini (2 inches/5 cm), 15 to 18 minutes

   small (3 inches/7.5 cm), 18 to 20 minutes

   medium (4 inches/10 cm), 22 to 25 minutes

   large (9 inches/23 cm), 25 to 30 minutes

Times can vary according to the thickness of the dough. For best results, rotate the pan(s) halfway through baking.

6. Remove from the oven, let cool in the pan(s), and then gently remove from the pan(s). A larger crust can remain in the pan till filled and/or served, to protect the crust from breaking.

Italian Baguette Sandwiches

INGREDIENTS

For the baguettes:

1 recipe Pâte à Choux (page 74)

1 large egg plus 1 tablespoon water, for the egg wash

Coarse salt and/or other toppings, such as poppy seeds or sesame seeds (about ¼ cup)

Fillings:

8 ounces (225 g) thinly sliced deli turkey

2 ounces (55 g) sliced pepperoni

2 ounces (55 g) sliced salami

¼ small red onion, thinly sliced

8 large basil leaves

Olive oil

Red wine vinegar

Coarse salt and black pepper

SPECIAL EQUIPMENT

Large pastry bag fitted with a large coupler only (no tip)

YIELD

4 large or 8 small sandwiches

METHOD

1. Make the baguettes: Preheat the oven to 425°F (220°C) and line a cookie sheet with parchment paper.

2. Place the prepared dough in the pastry bag fitted only with a large coupler. In a small bowl, beat the egg with the water to make an egg wash.

3. Pipe the dough in two 12-inch (30.5-cm)-long, 2-inch (5-cm)-wide strips, using approximately half the dough for each one. Try to space them at least 3 inches (7.5 cm) apart. Using a pastry brush, apply a thin layer of egg wash to each strip of dough. Sprinkle with coarse salt and/or other toppings.

4. Bake for 15 minutes, then turn the oven temperature down to 350°F (177°C) and bake for another 15 to 20 minutes or till golden and crispy. Remove from the oven. If the baguettes soften or begin to collapse within minutes of leaving the oven, they need to go back in for another few minutes to dry out.

5. When ready to assemble the sandwiches, cut the baguettes in half lengthwise. Remove the tops and begin to layer the meat one slice at a time, piling it high. Next, layer the red onion slices and basil leaves in a decorative manner. Drizzle with oil and vinegar, then sprinkle with salt and pepper. Slice the sandwich as desired.

NOTE

Baguettes can be stored, wrapped in plastic, overnight. However, they will soften. Alternatively, you can pipe the dough and freeze till solid, then transfer to a freezer bag for storage. The baguettes can be baked straight from the freezer.

Bacon & Chive Pancakes with Crab & Savory Sabayon

INGREDIENTS

For the pancakes:

2⅓ cups (240 g) almond flour

½ cup (60 g) arrowroot flour

½ teaspoon baking soda

½ teaspoon salt

5 slices crispy fried bacon, chopped, plus more for garnish

¼ cup chopped fresh chives, plus more for garnish

6 large eggs

½ cup (120 ml) milk of choice

1 teaspoon lemon juice

For the sabayon:

2 large egg yolks

¼ cup (60 ml) brut champagne

2 teaspoons finely chopped fresh chives

Salt and black pepper

½ pound (225 g) crab meat pieces, warmed, for topping the pancakes

SPECIAL EQUIPMENT

Candy thermometer

YIELD

Ten 5-inch (12.75-cm) pancakes

METHOD

1. Make the pancakes: In a small bowl, whisk together the flours, baking soda, and salt till blended. Add the bacon and chives and toss to coat.

2. In a separate bowl, whisk together the eggs, milk, and lemon juice till well combined. Add the flour mixture and whisk just till smooth.

3. Preheat a seasoned skillet (preferably cast iron) over medium heat. When it's hot, pour in about ⅓ cup (80 ml) of the batter. It will spread to about a 5-inch (12.75-cm) circle. Cook the pancake till the top starts to form small bubbles, about 1 minute, then flip it over with a thin metal spatula. Cook till it puffs up and sets, another minute or so. Repeat with the remaining batter. If desired, keep the pancakes warm in a 250°F (120°C) oven till all of the pancakes are finished.

4. Make the sabayon: In a medium-sized heatproof bowl, whisk together the egg yolks and champagne till frothy. Fill a small pot with about 2 inches (5 cm) of water and bring it to a simmer over medium-low heat. Set the bowl over the water, making sure the bottom doesn't touch the water. Using a hand mixer or an immersion blender fitted with a whisk attachment, beat the sauce on low speed till it becomes thick, voluminous, and warm to the touch, 7 to 10 minutes. (You can also whisk the sauce by hand, but it will be less voluminous.) When ready, it should read between 145°F and 160°F (63°C and 71°C) on a candy thermometer.

5. Stir in the 2 teaspoons of finely chopped chives and season with salt and pepper to taste.

6. To serve, stack the pancakes as desired, then top with the warmed crab meat and a generous amount of sauce. Garnish with more bacon and chive pieces.

Photo Instructions

MAKING CHOUX PASTRY

1. In a medium-sized bowl, whisk together the flours, sugar, and salt (not pictured). In a small saucepan over medium heat, melt the shortening, coconut milk, and water.

2. Once the shortening has melted, continue to heat the mixture till a few bubbles just break the surface. Do not let it boil. This step will determine how many eggs you will end up needing later, as the heat of the mixture will affect the absorption rate of the arrowroot and the evaporation of the water. You may need more or less egg in the final phase to get the desired consistency of dough.

3. Remove from the heat and pour the flour mixture into the hot milk.

4. Immediately stir, slowly at first to incorporate the flour, then vigorously till the mixture forms a big, soft blob of dough.

5. Transfer the dough to a stand mixer fitted with a paddle attachment. Stir on low speed for about a minute to cool it down. While the mixture is cooling, beat one of the eggs in a small bowl or measuring cup and set aside.

6. Turn the mixer up to medium speed and add one egg at a time to the dough, beating each egg before adding it. Allow each egg to be completely incorporated before adding the next, as the dough will break or separate with each addition. After adding the first three eggs, increase the speed and beat for about a minute or till the dough smooths out. Add more beaten egg a little at a time till the dough is creamy looking and reaches the desired consistency. To determine the ideal consistency, take a little dough between your index finger and thumb. You should be able to pull it into soft, sticky threads. The best way I can describe the texture is that it should be like chewing gum on a hot sidewalk (not pictured).

7. If piping, place the pastry bag (fitted with the tip) in a large glass and let the flap hang over the side. Using a rubber spatula or spoon, transfer the dough to the bag. This will save you a potentially big mess. Otherwise, use a mechanical scoop or spoon as instructed in the recipe.

8. Pipe or scoop the dough into rounds for cream puffs, oblong shapes for éclairs, or any other shape desired.

Tip: Choux can be a little finicky, because the amount of egg needed depends on how much water evaporates when the milk and fat are heated. You want the consistency to be thick enough not to spread out all over the pan and to maintain some of its shape. But if it's too thick, it may not puff up. Slight spreading is expected, though. As little as a teaspoon of egg can mean that it's perfect or too runny.

PIPING ÉCLAIR SHELLS

1. Start by marking guidelines on the back of the sheet of parchment paper you will be using, or place another sheet over the guideline sheet if you want to use it more than once. To do this, draw two sets of parallel lines lengthwise on the parchment paper. The distance between the lines should be the length you want your éclair shells to be, and the two sets of lines should be spaced at least 1 inch apart.

2. Use a large pastry bag fitted with a ½-inch (1.25-cm) plain tip to pipe the dough between the guidelines. Use smooth, upward movements as you pipe. As you finish each éclair shell, release pressure and pause for a moment before lifting the tip away.

For petite éclair shells: Pipe the dough into approximately 3-inch (9-cm)-long, 1-inch (2.5-cm)-wide logs. Space them about 2 inches (5 cm) apart.

For large éclair shells: Pipe the dough into approximately 5-inch (12.75-cm)-long, 1-inch (2.5-cm)-wide logs. Space them about 2 inches (5 cm) apart.

3. Gently brush each piped éclair shell with egg wash.

4. Use a dampened finger to smooth out any bumps in the dough, but do not press down or squish the dough.

MAKING CANDIED BANANAS

1. Slice the bananas lengthwise into ⅛-inch (3-mm) strips.

2. Lay the slices on a pan or piece of parchment paper.

3. Sprinkle the bananas generously with maple sugar.

4. Use a kitchen torch to caramelize the top of each banana. Use as desired.

Tip: Green-tipped bananas work best, as they are firmer and brighter tasting.

BUILDING CROQUEMBOUCHE

1. Have on hand a foam floral cone, parchment paper, scissors, and Scotch tape.

2. Roll the cone in the parchment paper, starting at the long end.

3. Tape the seam of the paper to secure it around the cone.

4. Trim the overhang of paper at the bottom edge of the cone.

5. Set the covered cone up on the base that you plan to use, then place some of the choux buns around the base of the cone to get an idea of how they will fit around the cone and to ensure that the assembled croquembouche will fit on the base. Then transfer the cone to a large piece of parchment paper laid out on your work surface.

6. Once the choux buns are filled, prepare one batch of the caramel glaze.

7. Dip the top of each bun into the caramel, then dip half of them in the coarse sugar, if using. Place them caramel side up on a sheet of parchment paper and leave to harden.

8. Prepare the second batch of caramel glaze while the caramel is setting. Dip the side of one bun into the caramel and stick another bun to it. Place at the base of the cone with the hardened caramel facing outward. Repeat with additional buns, placing the buns dipped in coarse sugar (if made) at random, wrapping them closely around the cone till the base layer has been completed. Repeat this process, adding tiers. Offset the buns using caramel everywhere they touch each other till you've used all the buns or you've reached the top of the cone. Make sure that the buns are being glued to each other and not to the parchment-covered mold. Leave the assembled croquembouche in place till the caramel is hard and set.

9. Carefully unmold the croquembouche by lifting it off the parchment paper, putting as little inward pressure on it as possible, as it can be fragile. Gently place it on your base for serving. If desired, once it's on the serving dish, you can add a few more filled buns to bring the croquembouche to a point.

Tip: If the caramel glaze starts to thicken too much while you're building, gently rewarm it for a few moments over the heat. Do not stir it, and do not let it boil.

ASSEMBLING PRALINE PARIS BREST

1. Draw an 8-inch (20-cm) circle on a sheet of parchment paper. I like to use a cake pan for this, but anything 8 inches (20 cm) in diameter will work. Flip the parchment paper over and place it on a cookie sheet.

2. Using a pastry bag with a round tip, pipe a circle of dough around the guide.

3. Pipe another circle inside the first one, making sure they are touching.

4. Pipe one more circle on top of the first two circles.

5. Make an egg wash by beating together the egg and water. Coat the whole ring lightly with the egg wash.

6. Sprinkle almonds evenly over the choux ring. Bake on the lower rack of the oven for 15 minutes. Move to the middle rack, then turn the oven temperature down to 350°F (177°C) and bake for another 20 minutes or till golden and crisp. Remove from the oven and let cool on a wire rack.

7. Using a large serrated knife, slice the ring in half horizontally to create two thin rings. Using a pastry bag with a star or French tip, pipe the pastry cream decoratively into the bottom half of the ring. Then, using a clean pastry bag and the same tip, pipe the whipped cream on top. Arrange the raspberries in a ring on top of the whipped cream.

8. Place the top half of the pastry ring on top of the bottom half.

9. Dust with powdered sugar if desired. Serve right away.

ROLLING OUT ALMOND FLOUR CRUSTS

For 9-, 4-, and 3-inch (23-/10-/7.5-cm) pans:

1. I like to start by fitting my rolling pin with silicone rolling guides (using the ⅛-inch/ 3-mm guides). These guides ensure an even and perfect thickness of the dough. They are readily available at most baking stores and online.

2. Place the round of dough on a large piece of parchment paper, lightly dusted with arrowroot flour to help prevent sticking.

3. Flatten the round of dough with your hands.

4. Dust the surface of the dough with arrowroot flour to help prevent sticking, then place another sheet of parchment paper on top.

5. Roll out the dough between the two sheets of parchment paper into a ⅛-inch (3-mm)-thick round. Then slide the dough onto a large cookie sheet.

6. Chill the rolled-out dough in the freezer for about 5 minutes or till the top sheet of parchment paper peels off easily. Do not chill it for too long, though; you want the dough to be flexible enough to shape into the pan(s). Peel off the top sheet of parchment. If it doesn't come off easily, place the dough back in the freezer for a few more minutes, especially if the room in which you are working is very warm.

7. Gently flip the dough over a 9-inch (23-cm) tart pan or, if using the smaller 4- or 3-inch (10- or 7.5-cm) pans, set three or four pans close together, flipping the dough over all of them at once. Carefully peel off the second sheet of parchment paper.

8. Use your fingers to maneuver and press the dough into the pan. Use pieces of excess dough to finish off the edges and fill in any cracks and tears.

9. Gently prick the dough all over with a fork.

FROSTING NEAPOLITAN CAKE

1. Frost the whole cake with an even coat of frosting, reserving most of the frosting for decorating. It's okay if a little cake shows through here and there; it will be covered later. Pay special attention to the top of the cake, though, using extra frosting and smoothing it out or giving it the texture you want the finished cake to have.

2. To decorate, fill a pastry bag with the remaining frosting and pipe a row of five or six dots down the side of the cake.

3. Place the tip of an offset spatula or butter knife against the middle of the first dot. Tilt the handle slightly toward the cake and pull some of the icing with the spatula to create a "petal" with a thin edge.

4. Repeat this process with the rest of the dots, then start another row of dots at the end of the row you just pulled. Continue making rows of dots till the whole cake is covered.

5. (Not pictured) For the top of the cake, pipe one layer of dots around the circumference, pulling them toward the center of the cake. Use a damp towel to clean any frosting off the serving plate.

ASSEMBLING OPERA CAKE

1. Place the first layer of trimmed cake in the center of a cookie sheet. Using a pastry brush, soak the cake in coffee syrup.

2. Spread about ½ inch (6 mm) of buttercream evenly over the surface of the cake.

3. Apply the next cake layer, then soak it in coffee syrup.

4. Spread the ganache over the cake in a thin layer.

5. Apply the next layer of cake and soak it in coffee syrup.

6. Add another layer of buttercream. Don't worry if it's a bit sloppy at the edges; this will be trimmed later.

7. Place the last cake layer on top and soak it in coffee syrup.

8. Apply a very thin layer of buttercream—just enough to fill in any pits in the cake to make a smooth base for the final chocolate glaze. Make it as smooth as possible.

9. Make the chocolate glaze: Heat the chocolate and shortening in a bowl over simmering water, stirring till just melted (not pictured). Pour it into the center of the cake and use a spatula to spread it outward to cover the top of the cake.

ASSEMBLING CAKE ROLLS

1. Lay out a large flour sack towel on your work surface. Using a small sifter, dust the surface of the towel generously with powdered sugar.

2. As soon as you remove the joconde cake from the oven, loosen the edges with a sharp knife.

3. Turn out the cake onto the sugar-dusted towel.

4. Carefully peel off the parchment paper.

5. With the short end of the cake facing you, immediately roll up the cake in the towel, rolling away from you. Let cool completely before filling.

6. When ready to assemble the cake roll, carefully unroll the cooled cake toward you. To help prevent it from cracking, gently lift the cake and support the back. Spread the filling over the top, leaving about a ¼-inch (1.25-cm) margin around the edges. This way the filling won't squeeze out the sides when you reroll the cake.

7. If using berries or fruits, sprinkle them evenly over the surface of the filling.

8. Carefully reroll the cake, using the towel to help guide the cake into a nice even roll. Refrigerate for about 30 minutes before glazing.

9. If the towel sticks to the cake, gently work it away from where it is sticking and continue rolling. Then place the cake on a wire rack to prepare for glazing.

ASSEMBLING BAKED ALASKA

1. To make the ice cream cake easier to remove from the bowl, line the bowl with plastic wrap, letting it hang over the edges.

2. Scoop about ½ cup (120 ml) of softened lemon curd ice cream into the bowl. Smooth the top, then put the bowl and the remaining lemon curd ice cream in the freezer for about 30 minutes.

3. Meanwhile, soften the strawberry ice cream, then scoop about 2 cups (475 ml) on top of the lemon curd ice cream in the bowl. Smooth the top and put it back in the freezer for another 30 minutes.

4. Soften the lemon curd ice cream again and scoop about 2 more cups (475 ml) on top of the strawberry ice cream.

5. Fit the trimmed cake layer on top, making sure that it sticks to the ice cream. Cover with plastic wrap and freeze for about 6 hours.

6. To make the cake easier to remove from the bowl, slightly warm the outside of the bowl with a hot, wet towel.

7. To remove the ice cream cake, pull on the overhanging plastic wrap till the cake releases. If the ice cream has become soft, wrap up the cake and put it back in the freezer for a few hours or till ready to use. The cake needs to be frozen solid; otherwise, the meringue won't stick to the cake.

8. When you're ready to serve the cake, make the meringue. Use a spoon or an angled spatula to decoratively cover the cake with the meringue.

9. Use a kitchen torch to caramelize the outside of the meringue. Serve immediately.

MAKING A DRUMSTICK HOLDER

1. Take an old egg carton, turn it upside down so that the molded part is facing up, and then, using a sharp serrated knife, cut about ½ inch (6 mm) off the tips.

2. Set the carton on end and, if needed, shave off a little more to get a good fit and remove any stray pieces.

3. After rolling the cones, place them in the egg carton with the pointy part down. Leave till completely set and cool.

4. Once the cones are filled with ice cream, they can be placed in the carton while the ice cream is freezing and again after the cones have been dipped and rolled.

MAKING MARSHMALLOWS

1. Grease an 8-inch (20-cm) square pan and line it with parchment paper, leaving some length on both sides to use as handles when removing the finished marshmallows. Dust the parchment with a light layer of arrowroot flour.

2. Place ½ cup (120 ml) of the water in the bowl of a stand mixer, then sprinkle the gelatin evenly over the water. Stir to combine if needed. Leave the gelatin to bloom while you prepare the rest of the recipe.

3. Combine the remaining ½ cup (120 ml) of water, maple syrup, and salt in a medium-sized saucepan. Bring the mixture to a boil over medium-high heat. Watch it closely, as it tends to foam up.

4. Place a candy thermometer in the mixture and continue to boil till it reaches 240°F (114°C). This usually takes 12 to 15 minutes after the first boil, but times can vary.

5. Secure the bowl to the stand mixer fitted with the whisk attachment. With the mixer running at medium-low speed, pour the hot syrup into the bowl in a slow, steady stream. Be sure that it melts all of the gelatin mixture. Try to avoid hitting the whisk or you will fling syrup all over the bowl.

6. Turn the mixer up to high speed and continue beating till the mixture nearly triples in volume and the marshmallow crème is just cool to the touch. This usually takes 5 to 7 minutes, or longer if using a hand mixer.

7. To check whether the marshmallow crème is ready, stop the mixer and lift up the whisk. The mixture should fall slowly off the whisk, like lava, before melting back into itself. Beat in the vanilla till just combined.

8. Transfer the marshmallow crème to the prepared pan, using a rubber spatula to clean the bowl. The crème should fill the pan about two-thirds full. Working quickly, smooth the top with an offset spatula.

9. Dust the top with a light layer of arrowroot flour. Leave to set, uncovered, for at least 4 hours. If leaving overnight, cover the pan with a light flour sack towel. Lift the marshmallows from the pan and cut into 1-inch (4-cm) squares or the desired size. Lightly toss with more arrowroot flour. I like to place the coated marshmallows in a fine-mesh strainer and shake off any excess coating for a smooth finish.

PIPING GRISSINI

1. Using a pastry bag, pipe the prepared dough into 12-inch (30.5-cm)-long and about ½-inch (1.25-cm)-wide lines on two cookie sheets. Space them slightly less than 1 inch (2.5 cm) apart. A standard cookie sheet should fit approximately 12 to 15 lines.

2. For the best shape, make both ends slightly larger than the rest of the grissini. Keep the piping bag moving at a steady pace, using even pressure to push the dough out. If you have holes because of air bubbles, just fill them in with a small amount of dough. The knobbiness makes them look more rustic anyway.

3. Using a pastry brush, lightly wet the top of each grissini with the egg wash.

4. Sprinkle the grissini lightly with salt and/or other toppings as desired.

Special Thanks

Ben: How do you say "thank you" to someone who is so intimately involved in the creation of something that the final product is as much a reflection of him as it is of yourself? It goes without saying that we share an uncommonly close relationship, but that dynamic alone doesn't fully communicate how much of this book exists because of you. In every photo, every recipe…in all the stories behind this mad creation, there's no discernible place where you stop and I start. To say "you support me" would be too cheap of a sentiment. To say "I couldn't have done this without you" would be the most foolish of understatements. I know that you refuse to accept any of the credit for this book, but I'll stand by this statement for the rest of my life: The cover of this book should have said, "By Jenni and Ben Hulet."

Oscar & Linus: My boys…the unsung heroes of this entire process. You are men among boys. You've held up photography props for hours at a time and held down the fort when I was too busy to cook or clean or do our laundry. You've demonstrated the kind of compassion and patience that are well beyond your years, and someday, a long time from now, you're both going to be the kind of husband that most people don't even believe exists. You will always be my greatest accomplishments.

Susan Hulet: The invisible force that has held our family together in a million uncelebrated and intangible ways. Without your constant availability and support, I doubt that this book could have happened. I'm positive that my boys would not have handled this whole process as well as they did without so much awesome Mimi time.

Wendy Moss: You believed in me from the very first time we met at yoga class. I have such an incredible amount of respect for you, and I can't tell you what it means to me that you've always shown such an unwavering belief that I would succeed. Your encouragement and generosity are two of the main reasons I even dreamed that I could do this.

Bill & Hayley Staley: Without you guys, this book would quite literally never have happened! Thank you both for believing in me, encouraging me, having Skype calls to answer my questions, telling me that I'm not losing my mind, reminding me that this would come together, and not letting me give up. The friendship that we've developed over the last year is one of the best things to have come from me writing this book.

George Bryant: Here's a truth—it's a great thing to know that George is in your corner. Thank you for your friendship, encouragement, and support throughout this blogging and book-writing journey. A huge factor in my deciding to do this book was having the Kickstarter succeed, and I know for a fact that it absolutely would not have been such a win for us without you championing it past the finish line.

Tami Finke: For being my champion, cheerleader, and friend. Your encouraging messages, surprise care packages, and ever-joyful spirit have been a constant light for me in the most difficult days.

The Victory Belt Team: Throughout this process I've met a surprising number of people who have also written books, and there's one thing that has consistently shown itself to be true. When I tell them what it is like to work with my publishing team—how they communicate, the kind of creative freedom I have, how they've handled setbacks and struggles—without fail those people are literally stunned and can't believe that it's true. I know I've never done a book before, but based on the overwhelming response I've seen to how you guys do things, I'm positive that I will never publish a book with anyone else.

TO OUR CREATIVE COLLABORATORS:

Matt Wagner & Felipe Trevino: For taking an idea and turning it into a video that told my story and inspired a host of people to support the Kickstarter that made this book a reality.

Chris Flynn: For helping me take a broad creative vision and distill it down into a simple canvas that could hold all my creative ideas. And for making me look good with your mad Photoshop skills.

Robert Milam: For lending your impeccable taste and keen eye to help make this cover design everything I hoped it would be.

Ashleigh Amoroso: For being too cool, hosting me in your home, talking endlessly about photography and editing, and finally capturing the photo that graces the cover of this book. I'm truly honored by your creative generosity. Photo credits: front and back cover, cover flap, and pages 8, 144, and 146.

Jenna Day: For meeting me in the middle of the wilderness to capture this wild idea I had for a marshmallow shoot. Your photos made that dream come alive, and I'm so glad we got to collaborate on it. Photo credits: pages 220, 221, 224, 240, and 241.

Meghan Cobb: For making me look like the most beautiful version of myself. You're an artist, and I'm honored to have your art as a part of this book.

TO OUR KICKSTARTER SUPPORTERS:

Talk about an awesome group of people! You guys believed in me and this book before we even knew where this road would take us. I didn't even have a working computer or camera when we launched our campaign, so the support that each of you lent is quite literally on every single page of this book.

Oreoluwatola Adesina
Israa Ahmad
LeAna Alvarado-Smith
Ashleigh Amoroso
Andrea Andersen
Michelle Anderson
Paris Anderson
Elizabeth Andrepont
Sonia Ardeel
Rena Arnold
Amy Ayers
Erin Badough
Michelle Baker
Julie Baker Riggs
Kathy Baldwin
Brandon Baralt
Belle Barber
Susan Basel
Alec Baulding
Tanya Beck
Jenna Bedingfield
Janette Bennett
Judy Benson
Gabriela Bernal
Elizabeth Berry
Orlane Bienfait-Luna
Thomas Booker
Sarah Bowen
Christine Boyer
Jennifer Brand
Stephanie Breznau
Summer Bronnenberg-Cano
Chrissy Brown
Colleen Brown
Jennifer Brown
Trent Brown
Daniel Brunsink
Elise Bryant
Sarah Bunk
Erika Burlock
Brandy Buskow
Angela Caisse
Fletcher Caldwell
Erin Callanan
Jennifer Calland
Lindsey Miranda Canaley
Brittney Carmichael
Tiffany Carra

Katie Cassady
Marianne Charters
Jessie Christensen
Aimee Christian
Odin Clack
Mindi Clark
Claire Clouse
Christina Coats
Jen Coelho Senecal
Joella Comp
Nicole Coneby
Lindy England Crain
Russ Crandall
Jen Crimaldi
Wendi Croft
Molly Cumming
Diane Davidson
Tabitha Davidson
Brandie Davis
Dianne Davis
Jennifer Davis
Marianne de Kleer
Pablo De la Fuente
Tawni Dean
Lourdes Delfin
Marcia DesRosiers
Rachel Dingwall
Michele Doherty
Tara Dotson
Bianca Downs
Katie Dreibelbis
Brett Duncan
Iris Eastburn
Dawn Eickhoff
Megan Eidson
Jennifer Egan
Cullen Elliott
Jennifer Anne Erickson
Donna M. Estrada
Amy Evans
Jennifer Evans
Michelle Fagone
Alysa Farrell
Tonya Ferguson
Tonja Field
Tami Finke
Amanda Fischer
Stacy Fischer

Niki Flaherty Wise
Amy Fox
Marie Frank
Amber Fritz
Jennifer Fuller
Nina Fuller
Christine Gannon
Catherine Garbus
Chandra Gaspar Achberger
Samantha Gaucher
Ami Gaudette
Denis Gilbert
Veronica Gilley
Matt Girgenti
Sheila Grady
Brittany Grant
Krista Grant
Kristi Hackenmiller
Paula Hagar
Lisa Hampton
Yvonne Hamrick
Cecilia Hanna
Alicia Hanson
Joan Harris
Madeline Hartman
Alyssa Heinrich
Stephanie Herriman
Anne Hess
Debby Hess
Amber High
Lindsay Holum Smith
Sarah Hornacek
Katrin Howes
Holli Hudson
Susan Hulet
Kim Jacaman
Ryan Jacobi
Jessica Jaeger
Brenda Jepperson
Ashley Denise Johnson
Libbi Johnson
Marta Johnson
Season Johnson
Lisa Johnson Mitchell
Alanna Jones
Emily Angela Jones
Billie Jo Kariher-Dyer
Roberta Karpinski

Melanie Karssenberg
Justin Katz
Lili Keeler
Hope Kerrigan
Erica Kerwien
KaHee Kim
Hallie Klecker
Nysa Kline
Pei-Ru Ko
Jeremy Daniel Kramer
Kelsey Krasnigor
Sherry Kratzer
Savanna Kreykes
Joy Lamb
Kristi LaMonica
Heather Lampert
Diana Lang
Alice Lau
Laurence Lau
Adam Lazur
Emily Leggett
Michelle Lemon
Bonny Lenz
Melissa Leon
Karissa Letchworth
Cheryl Lewellen Bond
Meg Lewis
Michelle Lewis
Roxanne Liedel
Rina Liles
Emily Long
Casandra Lopez
Lenore Ludlow
Heather Lynch
Brandi Mackenzie
Mandy MacLeod
Jessica Madieros
Valena Magill
Danielle Mahoney
Taunia Mann
Marianna March
Trish Marko
Lydia Marquez
Joel Martinez
Cali Matthews
Janice McAlister
Joi McClary
Emily McClernon
Renate McCollum
Donna McCullen
Brad McEntire
Andrea McGloin
Jen McIntyre
Judi McQueary
Lillian Mara Medville
Bridget Miles
Campbell Miller
Donna Miller

Rebecca Miller
Cristina Mladenka
Stephanie Moore
Kathlene Morales
Larry Morgan
Wendy Moss
Deneen Mueller
Michelle Muñoz-Alvira
Clare Narquis
Mike Nevotti
Angela Norbut
Jesse Nordyke
Amanda Oliver
Marilyn Olmsted
Chris Olson
Linda Parrillo
Kristin Parsons
Sarah Pearson MacDonald
Tanya Perez Ramos
Liza Pesenson
Stacy Pine Saunders
Gini Porritt Behrendt
Janet Potts
Heather Poundstone
Jen Puddick
Michelle Ramirez
Eden Rasmussen
Greer Rawlings Knox
Margaret Ray de Arenas
Tim Rayburn
Joelle Reynolds
Candace Ricciardi
Shelly Richardson
Jill Rickabaugh
Korina Riera
Joe Rignola
Garmisch Riley
Alyssa Rimmer
Kevin Robbins
Eileen Roberts
Stephanie Roe
Janelle Rooks
Hayley Rose
Annalissa Roy
Nicholas Rozier
Manon Ruel
Maggie Sammis Grayson
Jocelyn Sandruck
Goncalo Santos
Jennifer Sarduy
Maggie Savage
Sherrie Scaglione Castellano
Carolyn Scardino
Jessica Scholtz
Megan Schoof
Deborah Schumacher
Jean B. Schwartz

Naomi Scott
Sandra Setzke
Ingrid Shores
Nikki Siegel
Susan Silvestri
Kathleen Simis
Catherine Sis
Cheri Smilanick
Bethany Smith
Stephen Smyth
Asha Soares
Lucilene Souza
Michele Spring
Becky Steele
Heather Stegner
Teresa Stein
Monica Stephens
Rachael Stiles
Candi Summers
Vicki Swain
Andrea Swope
Kristin Szczenski
Mindy Taylor
Christy Teasley
Paulla Tewksbury
Amber Tomlinson
Angela Tong
Stacy Toth
The UDDA
Heather Uprichard
Kristin Vargas Nielsen
Catrina Vargas-Cormell
Carolina Villalon
Julie Waldman-Stiel
Beatrice Wallén
Anna Ward
Charlotte Warren
Beth Waltemath
Madilena Webb
Virginia Webb
Susan Welker
Erin West
Diane Wheatley
Rebecca Whitmire
Diana Wiehoff
Leona Wiehoff
Jessica Wilkens
Deb Wilson
Corwin Woody
Shari Wright
Emma Youngdale
Nida Zada
Sahar Zavareh
Jenny Zechiel Elledge
Zest Bakery
Catherine Ziegler
Daniela Zuzunaga

Resources

Though there are endless places to purchase the ingredients used in this book, here are a few of my favorite brands.

NUT FLOURS (CERTIFIED GLUTEN-FREE)

Honeyville: Blanched almond and hazelnut flours. Available on honeyville.com, at select Costco stores, and on Costco.com.
Nuts.com: Blanched almond, hazelnut, and pistachio flours.
Wellbee's: Blanched almond, hazelnut, and pecan meals. Available online at wellbees.com and Amazon.com.

ARROWROOT FLOUR

Authentic Foods: Available in health food stores and on Amazon.com.
Bob's Red Mill: Available in many stores and online at bobsredmill.com.

COCONUT FLOUR

Coconutsecret.com
Let's Do Organic: Available in many health stores and on Amazon.com.
Tropicaltraditions.com

SHREDDED COCONUT

Let's Do Organic: Available in many health stores and on Amazon.com.
Tropicaltraditions.com

MAPLE SUGAR AND SYRUP

Coombs Family Farms: Maple sugar and maple syrup. Available online at coombsfamilyfarms.com and Amazon.com.

FREEZE-DRIED BERRIES

Justtomatoes.com: Available in health food stores and online.
Nuts.com

GELATIN

Great Lakes: Grass-fed bovine gelatin. Available in many health food stores and online.

CHOCOLATE (DAIRY-, NUT-, SOY-, AND GLUTEN-FREE, NON-GMO)

Eatingevolved.com: 70% dark maple sweetened baking chocolate (fair trade) and cocoa powder.
Enjoylife.com: 69% dark chocolate morsels and chunk-style chocolate chips.
Equal Exchange: 70% dark chocolate chips (fair trade) and cocoa powder.

FULL-FAT CANNED COCONUT MILK

Naturalvalue.com: Great for basic baking.
Native Forest: Great for making whipped coconut cream. Found in many stores and on Amazon.com.
Whole Foods brand: Great for making whipped coconut cream.

COCONUT BUTTER

Artisana: Found in many health food stores and online at artisanafoods.com.
Tropicaltraditions.com (called Coconut Cream Concentrate)

SUSTAINABLE PALM SHORTENING

Spectrum: Found in many grocery stores and online at spectrum.com.
Tropicaltraditions.com

GHEE

Purity Farms: Available in many health food stores and online at purityfarms.com.
Tin Star Foods: Available online via primalfoodpantry.com.

Recommended Reading

Here are some great resources to further enhance your pastry-making knowledge. Many of these resources are not Paleo, although some of them are gluten-free. However, if you want to go deeper, much of what there is to learn about technique will cross over.

Joe Pastry (joepastry.com): A great place to learn terms and definitions as well as base recipes and other techniques. (Not a gluten-free blog.)

Pastry Pal (pastrypal.com): Another great place to read about technique as well as making your own almond flour and other ingredients. (Not a gluten-free blog.)

David Lebovitz (davidlebovitz.com): An excellent resource for techniques and recipes such as pastry creams, fruit curds, ice creams, and many naturally gluten- and grain-free French-style baked goods. (Not a gluten-free blog.)

Gluten-Free Girl and the Chef (glutenfreegirl.com): Here you will find some great gluten-free and Paleo recipes. This is an excellent place to get an introduction to going gluten-free, along with baking techniques. (A gluten-free blog.)

Tartelette (tarteletteblog.com): This blog is full of aesthetic presentation, photography, and food styling inspiration. There are also plenty of good gluten-free and even grain-free recipes throughout the blog. (Not a gluten-free blog.)

Cannelle Et Vanille (cannellevanille.com): Like Tartelette, this blog is filled with aesthetic presentation, photography, and food styling inspiration. You will also find great gluten-free recipes. (A gluten-free blog.)

Joy of Baking (joyofbaking.com): A helpful resource for information about egg sizing, weight conversions, cake pans, and more. (Not a gluten-free blog.)

Weights and Measurements Charts

LIQUIDS
(Water, Milks, Honey, Maple Syrup)

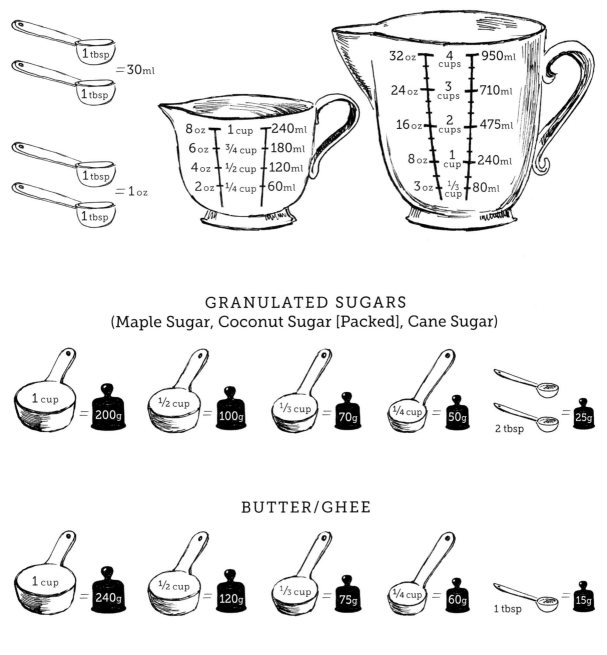

1 tbsp
1 tbsp = 30ml

1 tbsp
1 tbsp = 1oz

8 oz — 1 cup — 240ml
6 oz — ¾ cup — 180ml
4 oz — ½ cup — 120ml
2 oz — ¼ cup — 60ml

32 oz — 4 cups — 950ml
24 oz — 3 cups — 710ml
16 oz — 2 cups — 475ml
8 oz — 1 cup — 240ml
3 oz — ⅓ cup — 80ml

GRANULATED SUGARS
(Maple Sugar, Coconut Sugar [Packed], Cane Sugar)

1 cup = 200g   ½ cup = 100g   ⅓ cup = 70g   ¼ cup = 50g   2 tbsp = 25g

BUTTER/GHEE

1 cup = 240g   ½ cup = 120g   ⅓ cup = 75g   ¼ cup = 60g   1 tbsp = 15g

PALM SHORTENING

1 cup = 180g   ½ cup = 90g   ⅓ cup = 65g   ¼ cup = 45g   1 tbsp = 12g

NUT FLOURS

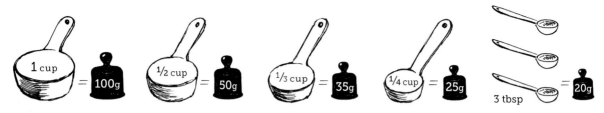

1 cup = 100g   ½ cup = 50g   ⅓ cup = 35g   ¼ cup = 25g   3 tbsp = 20g

ARROWROOT/TAPIOCA/COCONUT FLOUR/ POWDERED SUGAR

1 cup = 120g   ½ cup = 60g   ⅓ cup = 40g   ¼ cup = 30g   3 tbsp = 20g

SHREDDED COCONUT

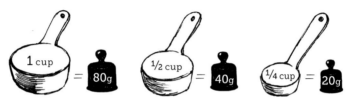

1 cup = 80g   ½ cup = 40g   ¼ cup = 20g

Allergen Index

EGG-FREE RECIPES

NUT-FREE RECIPES

Recipe Index

CHOUX PASTRY

Blackberry Almond Crusted
Éclairs (page 81)

Candied Banana Éclairs
(page 84)

Passion Fruit Meringue
Éclairs (page 87)

Matcha Green Tea
Cream Puffs with Ganache
(page 89)

Peaches and Caramel
Topped Cream Puffs
(page 91)

Espresso Cream Filled
Éclairs with Candied Bacon
(page 93)

Double Chocolate
Blackberry Cream Puffs
(page 95)

Croquembouche
(page 97)

Praline Paris Brest
(page 99)

TARTS

French Apple Tart
(page 111)

Citron Tart (page 114)

No-Crust Black-Bottomed
Banana Pies (page 117)

Mixed Berry Tarts
(page 119)

Frangipane Pear Tarts with
Chocolate Crust (page 121)

Mini Tartlet Combinations (pages 124–125)

CAKES

Chocolate Cherry
Naked Cake (page 137)

Neapolitan Cake
(page 140)

Sacher Torte
(page 143)

Chocolate Bundt Cake
with Blackberries
(page 145)

Vanilla Lavender Bundt Cake
with Vanilla Glaze
(page 147)

Opera Cake
(page 151)

(continued on next page)

CAKES (CONTINUED)

Raspberry-Glazed Vanilla Cake Roll /
Chocolate & Espresso Cake Roll (page 153)

Maple Carrot Cake
(page 156)

Tiramisu (page 159)

Madeleines (page 162)

COOKIES

Cinnamon Raisin Cookies / Cocoa Ginger Cookies / Snickerdoodle-Style Cookies (pages 171–173)

Italian Almond Cookies (page 175)

Extra-Thin Chocolate Chunk Cookies (page 178)

Chocolate Swirl Meringues (page 181)

Linzer Cookies (page 183)

Ladyfingers (page 185)

Maple Candied Bacon Blondies (page 187)

ICE CREAM & FROZEN DESSERTS

Vanilla Ice Cream / Strawberry Ice Cream /
Mixed Berry Sorbet / Chocolate Sorbet (pages 192–195)

Lemon Curd Ice Cream
(page 197)

Rocky Road Sorbet
(page 199)

Strawberry Lemonade
Baked Alaska (page 202)

Strawberry, Pistachio,
& Vanilla Layered
Ice Cream Cake (page 205)

Berry Sorbet Swiss Roll
Cake (page 207)

Linzer Cookie Ice Cream
Sandwiches (page 209)

Waffle Cones (page 212)

Cream-Filled Cannoli with Pistachios /
Double Chocolate Cannoli (page 215)

Pistachio Drumsticks
(page 217)

MARSHMALLOWS

Classic Marshmallows
(page 222)

Chocolate Marshmallows
(page 225)

Raspberry Marshmallows
(page 227)

Matcha Green Tea
Marshmallows (page 229)

Earl Grey Tea
Marshmallows (page 233)

Raspberry Neapolitan
Marshmallows (page 235)

Gingerbread Spice
Marshmallows (page 237)

Candied Bacon
Marshmallows (page 239)

SAVORY PASTRIES

Grissini (page 245)

Italian Pesto Pizza
(page 248)

Popovers (page 251)

Bruschetta Tart (page 256)

Italian Baguette Sandwiches
(page 259)

Bacon & Chive Pancakes
with Crab & Savory Sabayon
(page 261)

General Index